BHUTAN
1837-1838

BHUTAN
1837-1838

A REPRINT OF CHAPTERS XI, XII, AND XIII

(PAGES 197-312) OF

JOURNALS OF TRAVELS

IN

ASSAM, BURMA, BOOTAN, AFGHANISTAN AND THE NEIGHBOURING COUNTRIES

BY

WILLIAM GRIFFITH ESQ., F.L.S.

ASSISTANT SURGEON ON THE MADRAS ESTABLISHMENT, AND A SHORT TIME OFFICIATING SUPERINTENDENT OF THE HONOURABLE COMPANY'S BOTANIC GARDEN, CALCUTTA, AND SUBSEQUENTLY CIVIL ASSISTANT SURGEON, MALACCA

GYAN

Published by

GYAN

Gyan Publishing House
5, Ansari Road
Daryaganj, New Delhi-110002
Phone: 011-47034999, 9811692060
E-mail: books@gyanbooks.com

Distribution Network
gyanbooks.com
India, USA, Canada, UK, Australia, France

ISBN : 978-81-212-3147-3 (PB)
First Published, 1847

2nd Impression 2020

Printed at: Gyan Press, Delhi.

Bhutan 1837-1838
Author: William Griffith

BHUTAN 1837-1838

★ ★ ★

A REPRINT OF CHAPTERS XI, XII, AND XIII (PAGES 197-312) OF

JOURNALS OF TRAVELS

IN

ASSAM, BURMA, BOOTAN, AFGHANISTAN AND THE NEIGHBOURING COUNTRIES

BY

WILLIAM GRIFFITH, ESQ., F.L.S..

ASSISTANT SURGEON ON THE MADRAS ESTABLISHMENT, AND A SHORT TIME OFFICIATING SUPERINTENDENT OF THE HONOURABLE COMPANY'S BOTANIC GARDEN, CALCUTTA, AND SUBSEQUENTLY CIVIL ASSISTANT SURGEON, MALACCA

ORIGINALLY PRINTED AT
THE BISHOP'S COLLEGE PRESS
CALCUTTA
1847.

A COMMEMORATIVE REPRINT EDITION

PRESENTED TO

HIS MAJESTY
JIGME SINGYE WANGCHUK
DRUK GYALPO

ON THE AUSPICIOUS OCCASION OF

HIS CORONATION

1974

BY

CECILIA AND HALLVARD KULOY

CHAPTER XI.

Journey from Assam towards Bootan.

Left Gowahatti on the 21*st* and halted at Ameengong ghat.

December 22*nd*, 1837.—Left at twelve and proceeded to Hazoo, which is nearly due west of Ameengong, and distant thirteen miles. Road, through grassy plains; much cultivation throughout the greater part. Passed several villages, and forded one stream. Hazoo is at the foot of some low hills, on one of which is a temple of great sanctity with the Booteahs. The hills above this, as well as between this and Ameengong, abound with Cycas, many of which were once dichotomous; on these hills a fleshy Euphorbia likewise occurs, a sure indication of barren soil. Pea-fowl abound. The light-blue Jay figured in Hardwickii, Sterna, Haliætus pondicerianus, Chat, Butcher-bird, Edolius, Plovers, Hoopoe, and Ardea indica, were met with.

December 23*rd*.—Hazoo, a large village, extending nearly north and south, all the houses surrounded by trees. Areca bamboos, Ficus elastica, F. indicoides, F. religiosa, Sapotea (Mimusops) Arborea, Erythrina. Country to the east very jheely, and one huge expanse of paddy cultivation. Fine Loranthus, Hingtstha repens.

December 24*th*.—Nolbaree, seventeen miles nearly, N. by W., throughout the latter half of the way, the country consisted of highly cultivated plains, intersected by bamboo jungles, etc. Villages very abundant, surrounded by trees, especially bamboos. The hedges are made of a dwarf Pandanus. Crossed four streams, two not fordable. Grallatores and water-birds innumerable throughout, but especially after passing the Borolia, Bec ouvert or Anastomus coromandelianus, Pelicans, Water-hens, Divers, Ibis bengala, Cigoines (Ardea Pavonia) Syras, Mangoe-bird, large King-fisher, Hawks abundant, of which we observed five species; this is, generally speaking, one of the richest parts of Assam I have hitherto seen.

December 25*th*.—Dum Dummia, distance ten miles, direction north, country very open, in parts less cultivated than before, scarcely any jungle towards Dum; this is a straggling place on the banks of a small stream called Noa Nuddee.

The bamboo continues common, as well as Pandanus, Pterocarpus marsupium, Bombax, Diospyros ebenum, which are the most common trees. Villages are very numerous, but as usual, entirely concealed from view by jungle.

December 31*st.*—Up to this morning we remained at Dum Dummia, and had the Booteas alone been consulted, we should have remained there till to-morrow. It is a very uninteresting place, the country consisting of one extensive plain, diversified only by trees wherever there are villages. There is a good deal of cultivation, chiefly however, of rice; some sugarcane is visible, but it is of inferior quality, and evidently not sufficiently watered. Sursoo is considerably cultivated. The river Noa Nuddee is about seventy yards wide, with a stream of three miles an hour; it is full of sand-banks and of quicksands, and is crossed with great difficulty on elephants; by men it is easily fordable. The only shooting about the place is Floriken, which are very abundant, ten or twelve being seen in one day.

We left for Hazareegoung, a Bootea-Assam village to the north. We passed through a similar open country not much cultivated, but overrun with grassy vegetation. The path was of the ordinary description, and not kept at all cleared: crossed a small stream twice, with a pebbly bed and sub-rapids, a sure indication of approaching the hills. These, in their lower portion, have a very barren appearance, but this may arise from the cultivated patches: land-slips are of very frequent occurrence.

The grasses of the enormous plains, so prevalent every where in this direction, are Kagaia, Megala, Vollookher, Saccharum spontaneum, this is soft grass, and affords an excellent cover for game, Cymbopogon hirsutum, which is more common than the C. arundinaceum, Erianthus, Airoides, Rottboellia exaltata, Arundo, (?) Anatherum muricatum, Apluda, Trizania cilearis, is common in the old rice khets.

Among these occur a tall Knoxia, Plectranthus sudyensis, and P. uncinatus.

I observed Vareca, Grislea, about Dum Dummia. Elytrophorus is common in rice khets.

Towards Hazareegoung we came on a high plain, covered principally with S. spontaneum. Among this occurred Lactuioides, Premna herbacea, Grewia, with here and there Pterygodium. I observe here Bootea bamboo baskets made water-proof by caoutchouc; this is a practice much adopted by the Booteas: and the trees are here. The large coloured stipulæ are peculiar to the young shoots cultivated, they are often a span long. The young fruit is enveloped by three large coloured scales, which originate from the annuliform base; this is hence a peduncle, not a bracte, as I before supposed.

January 1st, 1838.—Halted.

January 2nd.—Marched to Ghoorgoung, a small village, eight miles from Hazareegoung and nearly due north. We crossed similar grassy tracts: the country gradually rising as we approached the hills.

Very little cultivation occurred. Crossed the Mutunga, now dry, but the breadth testifies to its being a large stream in the rains, as the boulders do to its being a violent one. The same plants continue; small jungle or wood composed of Simool. Trophis aspera, Cassia fistula, Bauhinia, Butea scandens, Byttneria, underwood of Eranthemum, and another Acanthacea.

About this place Cnicus and Arundinaria occur, and a small Santalaceous or Olacineous plant, with the habit of a Polygala. Merops apiaster is very common.

January 3rd.—To Dewangeri, distance eight miles.

Our route hither lay for the greater portion up the bed of the Durunga, the stream of which makes its exit about one mile to the west of Ghoorgoung. After ascending its bed for some time, the ascent becomes steep, for perhaps 800 or 1,000 feet, when we reached a portion of Dewangeri, but two or three hundred feet below the ridge on which the village is situated. The hills bounding the watercourse are very steep, many quite perpendicular, owing to having been cut away; generally they are of decomposed granite as at Dacanara, in some parts of conglomerate.

The torrent contains but little water, and very few fish, the banks are wooded tolerably well, as soon as the lower barren ranges are past.

At the base Cassia fistula, Leguminous trees, Artemisia, Simool, Spathodea, Bignonia indica, Sterculia, Cæsalpinea, Phlogacanthus thyrsiflorus, Pæderia fætida, Eugenia, Rhamnea, Croton malvæfoliis are found among the usual grasses, which form the chief vegetation.

These continue along the sandy bed for some time, but afterwards the usual small Andropogons usurp their place. Anthistiria arundinacea continue longest; with some of the large Saccharum, Rubus moluccanus soon appears, with Melica latifolia, and a species of Rhus.

Leptospartion is very common up to 1,000 feet, Pandanus 3-500 feet, but soon ceases; the higher precipices abound with an elegant palm tree, habitu Cocos.

Fleshy urticeæ and Aroideum become common at 300 feet, along the shaded watery banks, and continue so long as shade and humidity are found. Equisetum commences at 300 feet, Arundo, Saurauja, Pentaptera, which last ascends to 1,000 feet, as does Dillenia speciosa, Castaneæ feorox commences at 500 feet. Between this and the Choky, Polypodium, Wallichianum arboreum, Davallia grandis, Oxyspora, Musci, Goodyera, and Composita arborea are found.

At the Choky, the elevation of which is 965 feet, Œsculus begins. Wallichia,* Œschynanthus, Urtica gigas,* Derngia,* Govania,* Anthistira arundinacea, Alstonea, Angiopteris, are found. Grislea is found as high as 1,000 feet. Ficus obliquissima is found at 300 feet, and Ficus altera species as high as 700 feet.

At 1,200 feet Rubi sp., Panax, Cordia, are found, and on the steep ascent, Hastingsia,* Gordonia, Eurya, Corisanthera, Griffithia.

At one place the jack fruits, Ficus elastica, Compositi arborea, Panax altera species.

Dewangeri occupies a ridge 200 feet above our halting place, the elevation of which is 2,031 feet. The view to the north is confined to a ravine of 1,500 feet deep, at the bottom of which runs a considerable mountain torrent: to the SW. plains are visible, to the east and west the view is hilly.

The village itself is a poor one, containing perhaps sixty houses, but these are divided into three or four groups; the houses, with the exception of three or four stone and lime ones, are of the usual build, viz. of bamboo, and raised on muchauns. Filth and dirt abound every where, and the places immediately contiguous to the huts are furnished plentifully with various ordures.

Along the ridge three or four temples occur, these are of the Boodhistical form: they are composed entirely of slate, are white-washed; none are of any size, and the workmanship is rude in the extreme; on each face of the square basement, slabs of slate with inscriptions are visible, and in one instance many of these are ranged along a longish wall. The Pagodas are surrounded with long banners, with inscriptions fastened longitudinally to bamboos. On the west side of this the view is remarkably pretty, embracing all the temples, part of the village, and the Rajah's house. The hills adjoining being considerably diversified and remarkable, and for India over picturesquely wooded.

The pucka houses are ungainly structures, the height being out of all proportion to the width, the walls are very thick, and composed of slate slabs, the roof is choppered with projecting eaves, the windows are very narrow. Each has three stories, the middle one being occupied by the owner, this is divided into several rude compartments, each of which has one or two balconies.

The steps are rude and awkward, consisting of notches cut into large blocks. The cooking is carried on, on the ground floor, much to the edification of the residents above. Dirt abounds in every direction. The doors are rudely constructed of wood.

January 4th.—To-day was occupied by moving up into the village, in which we occupy a pucka house.

January 5th.—Visited the Sooba or Rajah, his house is very picturesque, reminding me much of the pictures of Swiss cottages: it is white-washed, with a red belt. The interior is capacious; the state room has hangings, which are decorated with native pictures on cloth. At the east end is a recess in which are some well-executed Chinese statues, the chief figure is of large dimensions, and is intended to represent the Durmah Rajah, whose statue is supposed to give infallibility. Two bells were suspended, one from the centre, the other from the balcony, the tongues of which were long, of ivory, and moved by a string. The Rajah received us in state, amidst discordant sounds of horns, pipes, and drums; his followers for the most part were badly clothed, the few decent looking persons being only decent externally. He was seated on a raised *dais* and was well dressed. He is a stout Chinese looking man, about 50 years old, and his deportment was certainly easy and dignified. The meeting was very friendly, but it is evident that we shall be delayed here at least seven days.

The central room in the Rajah's house is used as a guard house! arms were fixed round the walls, but they seemed to consist chiefly of spears, swords, and bucklers.

January 6th.—I walked this morning to a village, a mile to the west, in which there is a picturesque pucka house of religion. What pleased me especially was a specimen of a juniper, of extreme elegance, with drooping branches. The house itself was of the usual form, and one end was occupied as usual by an ornamental window and balcony. I noticed in addition Ulmus and Quercus.

The vegetation hitherto seen about this, consists of mango trees, several species of fig, among which were Ficus indica, elastica, terminalioides, Papyrifera, etc. two with cordate leaves occur. Ulmus,

2 *d*

Quercus, Bombax, Juniperus and Pinus, both cultivated. Aralia or Panax, four or five species, Croton malvæfolium, Justicia, Adhatoda, Peristrophe, Amaranthaceæ, Artemisia, Urtica urens? and heterophylla, Pogostemon, Triumfetta, (these occupy the old cleared spots,) Castaneæ sp. ? Artocarpus integrifolium, Erythrina, Sambucus ebulus, Rubi, three species, Solanum farinaceum, Engeldhaardtia, Pandanus, Leptospartion, Calamus, Nauclea, Euphorbia carnosa, foliis ligulatis, Artocarpus chaplasha, the fruit of which is eaten, Phlebochiton extensus, Sedgwickia cerasifolia, Callicarpa arborea, Porana, Randia, sugarcane, citrons, tobacco.

The fauna contains two or three squirrels, one of which is the small one of Upper Assam, Trocheloideus, the lesser Edolius or Drongo minor. Mainas, two kinds, carrion crows, Bucco, Muscipeta flammea, and one or two other species, Parus, two or three species, kites, large tailor-birds, sparrows. The black-bird of the torrents, and the usual water-birds, black pheasants; bulbuls very common, Bucco barbatus, parroquets, barking deer.

The temperature being 58° 61′, water boiled at 208°. The meanof two observations accordingly gives the altitude as 2,165 feet above the sea.

The number of houses is about 130, but these form two or three detached villages. The population is considerable, and there is no want of children. The people are stout and very fair, with ruddy cheeks, but abominably dirty. Some of the men are six feet in stature. We had one opportunity of witnessing their practice with the bow, but only two or three of the dozen candidates were decent shots. The mark was a very small one, and the distance 120 steps, but none hit it during the time we looked on, nor even the circular patch of branches, on which the slab of wood of this form was placed. The practice was accompanied with the usual proportion of noise and gesticulations.

There is very little cultivation on the hills around, so that this people are, at least about here, evidently dependent on the plains for their supplies. The cattle are a good breed, and totally different from those of the plains. Ponies and mules are by no means uncommon; there are likewise pigs and fowls, both of which are abundant, and of fine description.

January 16th.—Every thing leads me to conclude that the Booteas are the dirtiest race in existence, and if accounts be true, they are equally deficient in delicacy. Although much beyond other mountain tribes inhabiting either side of the Assam valley, in the structure of their houses, in their clothing, in their language, and probably in their religion, they are inferior to them in other points. Thus their looms are perhaps really primitive, and of the most simple construction; neither in their weapons of defence are they at all superior.

On the 14th I ascended a peak to the eastward, and certainly 1,000 feet above the village: on the summit of this, where there were the remains of an old clearing, I observed Pyrus, Acer, Rhus, Tetrantheræ, three or four species, Bigonia species picta, Carex, Composita arborea, Pteris aquilina, Kydia zyziphifolia, Saurauja, Eurya, Mæsa Panax, Artemisia, Hedyotis scandens, Callicarpa arborea, Camellia, Cælogyne, Oberonia, Otochilus fuscescens, Ficus, Cinnamomum, Æschynanthus, Pholidota, Cyrtandra, Piper, Citrus, Corysanthera, Hypoxis, Tupistra, Bambusa.

Sanicula appeared at 2,500 feet with Bartramea spectabilis, and a small Ophiorhiza, Acer at 2,800 feet, as likewise Rhopala; at 2,000 feet, Costus and Abroma, Thunbergia grandiflora.

January 19th.—I find that large quantities of Mungista or madder are sent to the plains from this, where the plant is very common; it is exchanged for ill preserved salt-fish, one bundle of madder for one fish. This fish is of an abominable odour, and probably tends to increase the natural savour of the Booteas, which, considering their total unacquaintance with soap, is sufficiently strong.

P. tells me that the Kampo country is situated north of this, and that it may be reached by a Kampo, in twenty-six days.

The language of the people we are now among, is distinct from that of Assam, as will be observed from the names given to the common grains cultivated in both countries, their principal grain is barley, which is of a fine description; very little cultivation being carried on here, the people drawing all their supplies from the plains. The following is a list of grains cultivated those marked* are Cerealea :—

	Assam.	*Bootea.*	
1*	Lalkonee dhan,	Yungra,	Panici sp.
2*	Legaid ditto,	Ditto,	
3	*Boot*, Tel,	Hnam,	A Sesamum.
4	*Cultivation* in Upper Assam,	Braime,	Polygonum Fagopyrum, grains very large.
5*	Bhobosa,	Khongpo,	Eleusine sp.
6*	Goomdam,	Peihnam,	Zea Mays.
7	Gellei-ma,	Linjee,	Phaseoli sp.

Ghoorgoung in Assam. ○ .—Santalacea, Gramineæ, Cnicus, Arundinaria, Cersium.

.—Cæsalpinia, Cassia fistula, Croton malvæfolia terminalia.

.—Palma sp. Phænicis ? trunco altiusculo.
.—Polytrichum aloides.
.—Rubus Moluccanus.

.—Polypodium Wallichianum, Angiopteris, Polypod. arboreum.

Chokey, alt. 965 feet. □ —Plectranthus cæruleus, Leptospartion, Œsculus.

.—Cordia.

.—Pogostemon. Rubus. Jasminum.

.—Bamboo, Jack, Ficus pyrifera, indica, elastica, etc.
.—Artemisia. Urtica urens, U. heterophylla, Justicia, Adhatoda, Phlogacanthus.
.—Sedgwickia, Quercus, Castanea 2, Bombax, Spondias.

Dewangeri, alt. 2,165 feet. ○ Rhus, Cordia, Cyrtandria, Æschynanthus, Artemisia, Croton malvæfol. Cupressus.* Pinus longifolia, Ulmus, Citrus 2. Saccharum, Rubia cordifolia, and munjista, Erythrina, Mangifera.

.—Clematis, Panax 4-5. Saccharum megala, Bolbophyllum, Costus, Abroma.
.—Thunbergia grandiflora.
.—Clematis, Exacum, Andropogon, Dicranum.

2,500 feet. .—Sanicula.

.—Acer, Rhopala, Eleocarpus.
.—Thibaudia.

.—Hypoxis, Orthodon.
.—Begonia picta, Pteris, Aspidum, Tupistra.
.—Acer, Pyrus, Kydia, Mæsa, Oberonia.
.—Cælogyne, Otochilus, Ericinea, Loranthus.

3,000 feet. .—Tetranthera, Artemisia, Citrus.†

The palm from the cliffs on the road hither is evidently a species of Phænix, pinnulis inferioribus spiniformibus reticula copiosa, pinnulis liniaribus acuminatissimus, apicem versus canaliculatis reticulo copioso, the height must be about that of a moderate Areca. No specimens of the trunk, none of flowers and seeds have been brought to me.

The temples here have a good deal of the Burmese shape, but the dome is more like that of a Mussulman mosque.

January 22nd.—Yesterday evening Mr. Blake's Khidmutgar died rather suddenly, he had been ailing for some days, but apparently not serious; his indisposition was owing to over-loading the stomach with radishes, &c. in which all partook too freely during the protracted halt, thus causing a good deal of sickness.

This place is so straggling that it is difficult to make a guess at the number of the houses, the greater number of the people are temporary residents and mostly are natives of Kampo,* they are more dirty than the Booteas, and seem to have an especial predilection for begging. When wishing to be very gracious they bow and gesticulate awkwardly, shewing their tongue at the same time. Their principal dress is coarse woollen clothes, and in lieu of turbans they wear caps or hats. Their beasts of burden are principally asses, which are perhaps from bad treatment, undersized: they likewise use goats, and largish animals between goats and sheep in appearance; of these we saw one male only, it had *once spiral* horns. Even a little black kid was not exempt from carrying its share, this was ornamented by woollen tassels of a red colour, fastened through a hole in the ear.

Pemberton tells me, that most of these people come hither with the view of going to Hazoo, a place of pilgrimage in Assam; some remain here as a security for the return of their brethren in three months, the period during which leave is granted by our friend the Rajah of this place. Their language is totally different from that of the Booteas. The day before yesterday an edict against catching fish, being taken off as I supposed it would be on shewing the Rajah some flies, Blake and I went down, and repeated our visit yesterday; the bed of the river at the debouchment of the path leading towards Tongsa, is elevated 1,431 feet, ($70.209\frac{4}{5}$), it is of no great size, and is generally fordable; the fish are almost exclusively Bookhar.† I saw one or two Sentooreahs,‡

* Eastern Thibet.

† *Barbus hexagonolepis,* Asiatic Res. xix.—Pl. f. 3, pp. 170, 313, 336.

‡ Cyprinus Semiplotus As. Res. xix.—Pl. 37. f. 2, pp. 274, 346.

and caught a long thin Bola,* beautifully banded with purplish-blue. The Bookhars as usual take a fly well, especially red hackles; the largest was caught by Blake, and must have weighed nearly three pounds.

Very little worth noticing occurred in the vegetation. Sedgweckia is common and of very large size, 2,400 feet above the river, as well as tree ferns.

Equisetum occurs in the bed of the river; in some places at the same level a species of Ranunculus, Aroidea, Succulent Urticeæ were common; along the edges or in the small churs, that have established themselves here and there, and which are covered with the usual Sacchara, but of smaller size; Erythrina, Leptospartion, Sambucus, Bœhmeria tomentosa, Kydia calycina, Grislea, Tupistra, Leea occurred, Ficus elastica is not uncommon, one specimen presented itself, which had sprung up on another tree, fifty feet from the ground; this it had destroyed, and the appearance was singular enough.

The juice is used for water-proofing bamboo vessels. The general rocks are slate, and this was the only one we saw *in sitû;* the vegetation is rather barren.

Near the bed of this river, which is called the Deo Panee, I found a curious Menispermous genus, Columnea, Clypeæ perianthia uncialata, ore integeriuscula, a Myrtacea, Uncaria, Abroma augusta, etc.

On ascending, Murraya exotica, Magnoliaceæ, Pæderia fætida, and Bignonia, occurred at low elevations, Lobelia baccata, Wulfenia obliqua, Costus, Chloranthus, Justicea orchidiflora below 600 feet, Eurya occurred scarcely below 1,800 feet with Millingtonia simplicifolia.

The cattle here are really noble, particularly the bulls; they are much like the Mishmee Methuns, but are distinct,† they are very quiet.

January 23*rd.*—Left at twelve, and arrived late at Rydang on a nullah, distant eight miles. Passed no villages, but passed a bridge erecting over the Deo Nuddee, at which place a Lam Gooroo or high Priest was employed: vegetation continued the same, and only two new plants occurred, a Stemodia with large yellow flowers, and a Begonia, with branched stems. Rydang is, 2,404 feet, above the sea (55.208½.)

January 24*th.*—Started early in the morning, (at 8 A. M.) the coolies mostly leaving at daylight. Yet although the distance was

* Opsarius gracilus, As. Res. vol. xix.

† See p. 35.

only eleven miles, we did not reach till 5 P. M. and many of the coolies did not arrive till late at night. The fact is the ascent was nearly uninterrupted during the day, the highest point traversed being about 6,000 feet. We then descended slightly to Khegumpe, our halting place, the altitude of which is 5,395 feet (46. 202,) at the highest point Fahr. thermometer stood at 42° at 1 P. M.

The first part of the road lay over grassy sparingly-forested hills, until we reached 4,000 feet. Here or a little below this the change in the vegetation commenced, the first elevational plants being Serissoid; Gaultheria, and Rhododendron commenced at about 3,600 feet on dry rocky eminences, which it always prefers.

On the 1st eminence, 600 feet above Rydang or 3,000 feet above the sea, Quercus, Castanea, Sedgwickia, Polypodium Wallichii, Lobelia, Pyramidalis, Composita arborea, Gordonia, Pteris aquilina, Anthistiria, Gramen airoides, Callicarpa arborea, Artemisia, Tephrosia, Flemingia, Govania, and these continued up to 4,000 feet. We here met with Kampo Tartars with their laden sheep, the children being generally placed cradle-fashion on the top of the loads, each in its own basket. Itea macrophylla, occurred at 3,200 feet, with Clematis, Hastingsia, Bignonia, Euphorbiacea, Briedleia.

At 3,300 feet Kydia zyziphifolia, Rhopala, Composita arborea, Hypericum,* Triumfetta, Smilax, Indigofera.*

At 3,600 feet, the same with Panax, Wendlandia, Myrtacea arborea, 1. Melica latifolia.

At 3,800 feet, Hedychium, Gaultheria, Habenaria, Serissoides, Gnaphalium, Gordonia, here very abundant, covered with Lichens and epiphytical Orchidea, Phyllanthus, Emblica.

At 4,000 feet, Rhododendron arborea, Eugenia, 1. Gaultheria arborea, Echinanthus, Bambusa, microphylla.* The same trees continue.

At 4,200 feet, Hedychium, Briedleia, Pyrus, Ficus,* and Rhododendron in flower, Gordonia, Itea macrophylla, Pteris aquilina, Osbeckia nepalensis, Artemisia major, Airoides, Flemingia.

At 4,500 feet, Myrica, Callicarpa arborea, Verbenaceæ, Buddlæoid,* Ardisia, Mæsa, Panax, Piper, Styrax, Camellia,* Polygonum rhæoides, Cyrthandra common, Mimosa arborea, Betula,* Ficus, foliis cordatis hispidis, Kydia calycina, Inga, Rubus moluccanus. Anisadenia, Begonia, Otochilus latifolius, Tussilaginoides, Neckeræ, Urticà, Gaylussacia, Lobelia, Panax, Æschynanthus venosus of Churra,* Lycopodium of Surureem,* Smilax ruscoideus,* Liparis, Rhododendron arboreum verum, Bucklandia of vast size. Hoya fusca, Ophiopogno,

Viola, Hymenophyllum, Croton heterophyllum Convallaria oppositifolia, Plectranthus Roylii, Begonia picta, Isachne, Cerastium, Spiræa, Hedera, Hypericum, Peliosanthes, Carex gracilis rupium, which commenced at 5,500 feet, Bambusa microphylla.

The forests here were damp and tropical so far as herbaceous underwoods were concerned, the trees were loaded with mosses chiefly pendulous Neckeræ and Hypnea, as well as the rocks; Epiphytes were common.

We then continued along ridges about the same elevation, Ranunculus, Hemiphragma, Thibaudia buxifolia, Polygonum rheoides, Pyrus indica. Gnaphalium common, Pteris aquilina, Airoides, Artemisia on sunny spots, Gaultheria, Galium of Churra, Arundo. The trees were about this all scraggy, but of picturesque appearance. Choripetalum, Panax, Laurineæ,* Piper, Cissus, Photinia and Gleichenia major, Thibaudia myrtifolia,* Potentilla, Calophyllum,* Hydrangea arbuscula,* Thalictrum majus,* Crawfurdia speciosa,* Macrocapnos,* Daphne papyrifera.*

Our march now wound round a huge hill with rocky head, lowering several hundred feet above us, the road being narrow, rocky, overhanging vast precipices. All the trees were scraggy, stunted with tufted grasses. Here about Dipsacus of Churra occurred, Buddleia, Phlomoides, Lonicera, Rosa, *Jubrung*, Cheilanthes dealbata of Brahmakund, Asparagus, Urticea arborea floribus fæm. capitulatis aurantiaces, Spirærea bella, Hymenopogon, Saxifraga ligularis,* on the rocks Primula,* in the crevices, with Hydrocotyla, Thalictrum renatum, Umbelliferæ,* Scirpus, Stemodia, Compositæ, Hypericum, Didymocarpus contortus of Oklong, Erianthus, Gymnostomum, all these on the bare rocks. Along the path, Codonopsis, Cnicus, Valeriana, Hardwickia, Lobelia

Hence we passed along nearly at the same elevation through romantic paths, the vegetation being European, and comparatively open: the trees covered with moss, with grassy swards here and there: the scenery was beautiful, the descent hence to Khegumpa was gradual and easy, along similar paths.

Noticed the following trees, &c. in the following order: Tetranthera, Gaultheria arborea, Tradescantia cordifolia,* Acer, Polygala, Deutzia, Tradescantia, Jasminum triphyllum, Plectranthus azureus, Macrocapnos, Rubia cordifolia,* Cucurbitacæ Cissampeloid, then forests of Rhododendron, on the paths Swertia, Potentilla, Fragaria, Alnus Acer folius palmatum lobatis oppositis, Porana.

This day I gathered about 130 species, the march was really delightful. The plants marked thus* indicate elevation.

Madder is furnished by both Rubia munjista and R. cordifolia, these species are quite distinct, the latter affecting greater elevations than the former, scarcely descending below 4,000 feet.

Scarcely any water occurred on the route; from just above Khe-gumpa, a beautiful valley is seen to the left, with a good deal of cultivation. No large villages were seen.

Rydang O altitude about 2,000 ft. * See section of route.—Sedgwickia &c.

.—Quercus, Callicarpa arborea, Euphorbraceous trees.

.—Gordonia covered with Epiphytes.
.—Hypericum, Lobelia pyramidalis.
.—Seressoides, Gaultheria, Gnaphalia, Habenaria.

.—Rhododendron, Thibaudia myrtifolia.
.—Bucklandia, Garcinia ? Eugenia.
.—Quercus lamellata.

.—Gaylussacia, Masdevallia, Otochilus major.

7,000 feet. .—Bucklandia, Lomaria, Otochilus major, Quercus lamellata.

.—Artemisia major, Gnaphalia, Arundo, Composita arborea.

.—Acer sterculiaceum, Rhododendron.
.—Scirpus, Umbelliferæ, Hypericum, Primula, Stemodia, Compositæ, Thalictrum.

.—Rhododendron.
.—Dipsacus Macrocapnos, Thalictrum majus, Cissus, Rubus potentilla folius, Treefern, Polypodium.
.—Woods with pretty glades and swards, Oaks, chiefly Bucklandia, Swertiæ.
.—Phlomoides, Viburnum. Spireaceæ, mosses abound.

Khegumpa. O .—Abies, Pyrus, Rhododendron, Lobelia, Viburnum, Potentilla.

January 25*th.*—Khegumpa. This is a pretty place; but the whole country has a wintery appearance from the trees having mostly deciduous leaves; it is a small village, not containing twelve houses. Pagodas with the inscription-bearing walls occur as usual; on a small hill rising from just below the village, a large house with out-houses belonging to a Lam Gooroo, is the prettiest bit of architecture I have yet seen. We put up in a small house, of the usual poor construction, capable of containing four or six people, the roofs are of wood, the planks being kept down by stones. The evening was very cold, but the thermometer did not fall below 44°. Here a solitary specimen of Pinus was seen.

A beautiful tree, with pendulous leaves and cones, which resemble those of Abies, occurred. Rhododendron is common here. Around the hut I observed Lobelia, Rumex, Quercus, Ranunculus, Plantago, Leucas ciliata, Gnaphalia, Rubus, Urtica urentior, Rubi 2, Pteris aquilina, Geranium, Galium, Artemisia major, Fragariæ, Betula? ramis pendulis, foliis lineari lanceolatis, *Jubrung*, Phlomoides, in flower, Spiræa bella, Tetranthera, Daucus, Gleichenia major, Oxalis corniculata, Dipsacus. The trees were covered with Lichens; the only cultivated plants I saw, and of these only straggling individuals, were tobacco and Bhobosa.

In a wood at the base of the hill on which the Lam Gooroo's house is situated, Saurauja hispida, and S. arborea,* Woodwardia,* Rubia cordifolia, Oaks, Spiræa bella, decomposita, Stemodia, Cerasus, Curculigo, Pogonatherum,* Carduus, Polygonum rheoides, Panax, Bucklandia, Berberis asiatica and Porana, occurred.

Our march, after passing this hill, commenced by a descent through a damp wood of Oaks, Eurya. Here Swertiæ 2 occurred on banks. Clematis verbesina, Gordonia, Erythrina, Myrica. Thence we passed along a ridge, the forests being stunted and wintery, abounding with Rhododendron and oaks. Myrica, and pendulous lichens occurred in abundance, but grasses predominate, chiefly Airoid and Andropogons.

From this to the right was seen a beautiful valley with a moderate-sized village and picturesque houses, with considerable and very clever cultivation.

Thence we crossed to the other side of the ridge, descending a little and then continuing through forests of oak, consisting of a species found on the Khasyah hills, and approaching Q. Robur: as all the leaves had fallen, the whole appearance was that of winter. Here I shot the Jay figured in Royle's work: continuing to descend very gradually, I observed Epilobium,* Neckera, Fissidens, Brachymenium, Nerioideum in fruit and half buried in the fallen leaves; a pretty Gentiana, Ruta albiflora, Potentilla. After passing along this for some way we commenced a sharp descent. At about 4,800 ft. Vitex simplex, occurred. Indigofera re-appeared, with Saccharum rubro nitens of Churra, the other grasses being Andropogons, 2-3, and Orthopogon, Hedychium, Gordonia soon re-appeared: to the east, cultivation was visible, and to the north, Pines were visible in every direction stretching away far below us to a considerable torrent. About one-third of the way down this steep ravine, at the bottom of which a torrent was heard roaring, Wendlandia, Spiræa bella, Hedychium, Gaultheria arborea, Aspera Rhododendron, Pteris aquilina, Artemisia, Saurauja hispida, Indigofera, Eurya, Mimosa arborea, Mæsa angustifolia of yesterday, Osbeckia nepalensis, Viburnum, Tetranthera, Ficus, Gleichenia minor, Crawfurdia speciosa, Polygonum rheoides, were found. Hitherto the woods had been dry, or rather so, but on turning to the east, we came into damp woods presenting many tropical features, along which we continued descending gradually for some time: at the commencement in this, Callicarpa arborea, a weeping Beech, Dipsacus verbesina, and the Alnus, of Thumathaya occurred, Arbutoideus, Hydrangea, Urtica heterophylla, Neuropeltoid aromatica. Then below we came on Piper, Deeringia, Cerasus, Sanicula, Cyrtandracea, Cheilosandra gracilis, and fleshy Urticeæ. Underwood, herbaceous forms of Acanthaceæ, Ferns, as Davallia, Asplenium, all more or less succulent. Darea, Glycine, Buchanania, Saurauja ferruginea, Thalictrum majus, Pothos, etc. Hypericum, Begonia, Panax terebinthaceus, Magnoliacæ, Garciniæ, Valeriana cordifolia.* Passing on at the same elevation, we suddenly rounded a ridge, and in one moment came on dry, sunny, rocky, grassy ground, the trees being exclusively Rhododendron, oaks and a few Gordonias with Airoid, Andropogons, Pteris aquilina: we then came on the brink of the ridge up to which Pinus longifolia ascends; the elevation of this was 4,132 feet (60-204½.*) From this all around Pinus is visible in profusion; we then dipped to the south, this face being occupied by thick forest, having Rhododendrons on the skirts. From the above spot Saleeka was visible, with a fine grove of Pines, it is 1,500 feet, at least above this.

* Such figures; may be thus read. Temp. of the air 60° Fah., that of boiling water 204½°

The descent was steep, we soon came on Callicarpa arborea, Celtis megala, Pogostemon, Stemodia grandiflora; this was about 4,300 feet, where a clearing had been commenced: close to this I observed Martynia, Pteris, Composita arborea, Desmodium vestilum, Flemingia, and gathered at 4,000 feet a Verbenaceous shrub, looking like a Plumbago, and a Bœhmeria; continuing, without descending much, I came on Pinus, Rhododendron, Gaultheria.

Loranthus was here a common parasite on Pinus, oaks occurred but the species was changed; this had small leaves, white underneath; and descending we continued through pine woods, Artemisia minor, together with the usual grasses and Aspideium macrosomum.

Here we travelled along a hill just above a ravine. Either side of this was covered with grasses and pines, the ravine being crowded with oaks, etc. Panax, and Composita arborea occurred.

A little below this, Hastingsia, common, Desmodium hispidisum, Artemisia minor, Briedelia, Mimosa, and several Compositæ: we continued descending very steeply, and observed Holcus elegans, Melica latifolia, Erianthus Apludoid Circium.

At 2,600 feet, came on Scutellaria; Pines had ceased, but on the opposite side of the nullah, they descended lower. Knoxia scandens, Kydia calycina, Hastingsia, Hedyotis linearis, Ficus pedunculis radiciformibus pendulis, Leguminous trees as Dalbergia, Truimfetta; Bœhmeria, Asparagus, Buchanania again, Solanum, 10-dentat., Urtica urens,—1. (66-208½.*)

The altitude of the bed of the Cameon nullah is here, 1,937 feet, its banks are formed by hills cut away and hence precipitous, those to the east are covered with Pines, Oaks descend to this. Here Arundo Karka, Leptospartion, Erythrina, Artemisia major, Solanum farinaceum, black pheasants of which I shot a male. Ficus Dumooriya, Grislea, Rhamnoid scandens, Pandanus, Bœhmeria torrentum, Urtica pendula, Barleria Prionites of Dgin, Sida cuneifolia, Dalbergioid.

Thence we ascended 100 feet or thereabouts, and descended to another and larger torrent. Anonaceæ, Phlogacanthus thyrsifloris here occurred.

The bed of this stream is 70 to 80 yards wide, but the volume of water is inconsiderable. The hills forming the opposite bank are lofty, not under 4 to 5,000 feet; their bases and the nullah above alluded to have the vegetation of Dgin, otherwise they are clothed with the

* See note p. 212.

usual grasses and noble Pines. The brown bird with crooked bill was heard here.

At 500 feet above the torrent Menispermum, Bidens albiflora, Megala, Leptospartion, Verbenacea, Plumbaginea, Mucuna, Desmodium hispidum and Ficus were seen as before: Phyllanthus, Emblica, and Grislea occurred at 800 feet: Grewia at 1,000 feet: and Osbeckia linearis occurred at 1,200 feet in rocky places; with Poa, Cynosuroides of Churra, and Bassia at 1,300 feet, with Emblica, Labiata sudyensis, Osbeckia nepalensis, Ficus.

On rounding the ridge to the east, which is 200 feet above this place *Sassee*, we came on a forest of oak, Rhododendron, Viburnum, Pothos pinnatus.

January 26*th*.—Sassee. Our coolies left us here, they are not very good ones, not equal to Khasyah, they are however merry, and whistle or sing when tired, their feet are generally naked, but occasionally they wear leathern sandals. Thermometer 60°: water boiled at 204½°: altitude 4,109 feet.

About this place I first met with Thlaspi bursa pastoris, Malva rotundifolia also occurs, Ligustrum, Adhatoda! Euphorbia ramis 4-gonis, foliis? in spinis abeuntibus! Bambusa, Urtica urentior, Geranium, Rumex of Khegumpa, Pancratium or Crinum! Peristropha triflora, Holcus elegans, Pteris aquilina both Artemisias, Panicum cynosuroides! Stemodium ruderalis! Callicarpa arborea! Cerasus, Pyrus indica and malus, Barleria prionitis! Ervum, Hedychium coronarioides! in wet places, Buchanania, Peperomia, Moschosma! Dendrobium! Thibaudia myrtifolia, Gordonia, Dioscorcæ! Tetrantheroid arbor magna, Pinus longifolia, Quercus, 2-sp. Rhus, Citrus also is found. Thus the mixture of forms is nearly excessive, those marked ! thus indicate usually low elevations. Rubia cordifolum.

The whole four leaves of this plant are petiolate, but one pair is perhaps always unequal, one occasionally abortive, I look upon this as a proof that the so-called stipulæ of Stellatæ are real leaves. There is this difference then between Rubiaceæ and Stellatæ, the one has covered buds, the other not. The development of the lamine before the petiole is particularly conspicuous in this plant.

Buck-wheat with trisulcate seeds, and Cannabis sativa are found here; barley is cultivated.

January 27*th*.—Sassee: temperature 58°, big metal thermometer. Tomato found here; Leptospartion ascends woody ravines as far as this; of birds, the larger dove is abundant; Verbena officinalis.

January 28th.—On walls about this a Lobelia, and Stemodia ruderalis occurred. Sassee is a ruined village, said once to have been large, now containing not more than five or six houses, an equal number being in ruins.

January 29th.—Commenced to descend almost immediately, until we reached the Giri Nuddee, we then ascended again 5,600 feet, and continued over excessively precipitous rocky ground, until we reached the nullah again.

The same vegetation continued until we had descended some hundred feet. Pinus, Quercus, Rhododendron, Viburnum, Indigofera, Osbeckia nepalensis, Desmodium, Gaultheria arborea, Rubus, deltoidifolius, Conyza, Saurauja ferruginea, Crawfurdia speciosa, Labiata sudyensis, Dipsacus occurs but is rare, Gordonia, Rubus idæus, Gleichenia minor, Pendulous lichens, Galium asparajus, Engeldhaardtia, Smilax.

The descent was steep. Thibaudia myrtifolia, Peperomia, Stemodia grandis, Airoid, Otochilus linearis.

At 300 feet Composita arborea, and penduliflora, Polygonum rheoides, Flemingia, and a cleared spot with Zea Mays. 400 feet Pteris aquilina, Rubus moluccanus, Aspidium Polypodioides, Lygodium, Aspidium macrosorum, Moschosma, Mimosa arborea, Millet, Cerasus, Hedyotis, Plectranthus, Roylia, Knoxia Scandens, Ruta albiflora, Rottlera, commenced at 500 feet. Stemodia, Hovenia, Cerastium, 4-ovulatum, Carex.

BOOTAN.

Khegumpa, 6,900 feet. O .—Abies, Tetranthera, Salix, Jabrung, Geranium, 6,900 feet Artemisia.

.—Tobacco, Dipsacus, Rumex,* Gnaphalium, Bhobosa.

Saurauja hispida. .—Thalictrum, Epilobium, Rhododendron, Panax, Berberis asiatica, Ruta albiflora.

.—Damp wood of Oak, Eurya, Laurineæ Swertiæ 2, Spiræa, Compositæ, Gillemoides.

.—Dry open ridges, rocky ground covered with Andropogonous grasses, Ichanthus.

.—Airoides, Conyzoid, Quercus, Rhododendron, Myrica, Cirrhopetalum.

.—Dry open wood composed almost entirely of Quercus, Roburiordes, Gentiana, Nerioides.

.—Rubi, Saurauja, Artemisia major, Saccharum aristatum.

.—Betula, Alnus, Arbutoides, Neuropeltis, Ficus.

.—Humid woods, *herbaceous underwood,* Acanthaceæ, Ferns, abundant.

.—Cheilosandra, Buchanania, Pothos, Urtica heterophylla, Cerasus.

.—Urticeæ abundant.

.—Dry open woods, rocky ground as before. Rhododendron abundant.

.—Pinus longifolia ascends on the western face thus far.

4,200 feet. .—Rhododendron, Quercus.

.—Humid wood, Celtis, Callicarpa arborea, Quercus, Eurya, Composita arborea, Verbenacea Buddleoid, Martynia.

.—Gaultheria.

Chilluree Nuddee, 1,937 feet. .—Pinus longifolia, Rhododendrons.

.—Mimosa, Pinus, Mæsa, Compositæ, Artemisia minor.

.—Buchanania.

.—Arundo, Leptospartion, Bœhmeria torrentum.

.—Anonacea, Phlogacanthus thyrsiflorus.

.—Callicarpa arborea.

.—Pinus longifolia, with grasses as before.

.—Verbena plumbaginea.

Ficus.

.—Berberoides, Emblica.

.—Round ridge, then again Pinus longifolia.

Sassee, 2,400 feet. O .—Rhododendrons, Oaks.

Carex, Kydia, Jujubifolia, Randia, Hovenia, occurred at 600 feet with Rhopala, Panax, Ficus obliqua.

Then shady jungle commenced, underwood of Ferns, Acanthaceæ, Urticeæ, Andropogons, Stemodia secunda occurred at 700* feet. Hastingsia, Pogostemon, Kydia calycina, Glypea, Curculigo, 750 feet, with Clematis Cana, Cerasus, Quercus Robur, this came down a ridge. Rhus acidissima.

Scleria, Lycopodia, Mæsa, Sterculia Balanghas, and Kydia Jujubifolia, at 900* feet. Phlomoides, Acanthacea specicosa, Pothos pinnatus, Choulmoogrum, Malpighiacea, at 1,000* feet. Buchanania, Magnolia, Achyranthes, Murraya exotica, Sedgwickia, Urtica Gigas, Chloranthus inconspicuus, Peliosanthes, Phænix pygmæa, Hedysarum acenaciferum, at 1,200* feet.

The altitude of the bed here is 3,112 feet (64, 206$\frac{1}{5}$: of Woollaston, 6.4.3)† and along its banks Cissus, Woodwardia, Megala, Polygonum Rheoides, Mimosa arborea, Curculigo, Woodwardia, Andropogon fuscum, Conaria, Potentilla, Rumex, Rubia cordifolia, Drymaria, and Begonia occurred.

The ascent was steep, leading over several land slips, the same vegetation continuing. Oaks, Pines, Rhododendrons occupying the more exposed faces, and the usual humid jungle characterising aspects not so much exposed. Pinus longifolia strays down to within 100 feet of the nullah. We passed a pretty cascade discharging a considerable body of water : here at 200* feet above the nullah, I observed Crotalaria juncea, the Betula of Thumathaya, Quercus lanatus, Leea crispa, Panax terebinthaceus, Indigofera, Scutellaria, Clematis, Cana, Panax altera, Mimosa, Porana, Arundo karka, Flemingia, Conyza, Aspidium macrosomum.

At 400* feet, Itea macrophylla, Ficus, Composita arborea. The woods are dry, but little occurring underneath the trees, except the usual grasses, Andropogons and Airoides. At 500* feet, Thibaudia myrtifolia, Triumfetta mollis, Composita penduliflora, Lysimachia, Pinus, Rhododendron. The ground now became excessively rocky, the road winding along at the same elevation, not more than a foot wide.

At 600* feet, Desmodium vestilum, Artemisia, Acanthacea lurida, Gentiana, as before. Gordonia, Bambusa, Microphylla, Arum viviparum, Tussilaginoid, Wendlandia, Thibaudia, *variegatoides*, and a myrtifolia; Sedum, rocks strewn in every direction covered with Sedum and epiphylical orchideæ.

* Relative heights.

† These figures refer to Woollaston's thermetrical barometer.

On rounding a ridge with a north-east aspect we came without altering our elevation, on a humid jungle. Pothos pinnatus and red, Ferns, Acanthaceæ, Choripetalum, Calamus, Acrostichea, Blakea, Grammitis decurrens, Moschosma. We descended through similar jungle with Pandanus also occurring until we again changed our aspect, when the oak woods, etc. reverted with Rhododendron and Thibaudia myrtifolia; again changing, we returned to an intermediate jungle, gradually assuming all the humid characters of those places passed before. Here I observed Tupistra, Asplenium nidus, at 200 feet above the bed of a nullah. Rottleria, Mimosa arborea, Crawfurdia, Speciosa, Zanthoxzlon triphyllum.

Along the bed of this nullah, Crawfurdia speciosa, Potentilla, Choripetalum, Eurya, Ranunculus, Cardamina, Juncus! Oxyspora, Saurauja hispida, occurred; some in a sort of marsh, with Thibaudia variegatoides. The places along which torrents formerly flowed were occupied by Typha elephantina, Kujara, Megala, Arunda, the Alnus of Bhailseeree, Artemisia major, Rubus deltoidifolia, (Corysanthera hispida with Juncus;) here Anthistiria arundinacea, Artemisia minor, Bucco grandis (Bird), Polygonum rheoides, Bæhmeria torrentum, Gaultheria deflexa, Indigofera, Oaks, Gordonia, Holcus elegans, Conaria nepalensis in flower, and Erythrina occurred along the bed, up which we proceeded about a mile.

We then ascended among Pines and Oaks, Callicarpa arborea, and others, ascending up the humid ravines, which in the rains give exit to torrents—at 300 feet noticed a different Pinus, which is observed in abundance on a mountain on the opposite side, up which it ascends 2 or 3,000 feet.

Callicarpa azurea, Buddlea Neemda, Eugenia, Serissoides, and the Saccharum of Churra, occurred here.

The ascent was continual but gradual, rounding the almost precipitous face of the hill, the path was stony, often loose and frequently not above a foot wide, with a precipice lowering above and yawning beneath. The vegetation had, with the exception of the Pines, Oaks, and Rhododendrons, all been burnt, so that the ascent was uninteresting. As we neared the summit it became bitterly cold, a strong biting wind nearly cutting us in two: we reached Bailfa, which is on the summit but sheltered, at 6 P. M.

Conaria occurs at the top! being more advanced in flower than below; in one instance with young capsules. I noticed Pogonatherum, Didymocarpus contortus, Serissoides, Gaultheria fruticosa, Polytrichum fuscum, gathered at 7,000 feet. previously: at 1,200—1,500 feet above the nullah, Indigofera reaches the top. In a sheltered place here I found a beautiful Gaultheria; a small Campanula occurs on the rocks at from 1,000 feet upwards.

BAILFA or *Bulphai*.—This place is 6,808 feet above the level of the sea, yet on the east and south are mountains towering far above it. Snow is said to fall in February, but sparingly—the hills around are bleak, thinly vegetated, except those on the south of the Geerea, which are more wooded. There are only a few houses. Turnips and barley are cultivated here, and in these fields may be found a Cruciferous annual, and probably a small species of Lamium. The chief cultivation is visible in the valleys below. Buckwheat is among the number.

January 29th.—To-day I sallied out a few hundred yards to the west, on turning over the ridge, the south side of which is so bleak, thinly covered with Q. lanata and Rhododendrons, I found myself in a thick shady jungle, the chief tree being a species of oak, widely different from Q. lanata. The trees and shrubs are loaded with mosses, especially pendulous Neckeræ, Daltoniæ, Hypne; Hookeria, Fissidens, etc. occurred on the ground. I imagine, I gathered twenty-five species of mosses here. Ferns were likewise abundant; I noticed Daphne papyracea, Berberis asiatica, Conyza nivea, Smilax ruscoides, Œschynanthus venosus, Hedera, Ophiopogon linearis, O. latifolius, Cymbidium veridiflorum, Ardisia crenata, Carex, Piper! Clematis, Gordonia, Spiræa decomposita, Composita volkamerifolia, Cissus, Smilax, Bambusa microphylla, Viburna, as before. Gaylussacia serrata and microphylla, the former in fruit. Thibaudia lanceolata, buxifolia, Gaultheria of yesterday.

On the exposed face Santalacea, Gentiana, Hypericum decussatum of Moflong, Leucas ciliata, Ischæmum pygmæum, on Rhododendron, Loranthus obovatus. The mosses of this side were Brachymenium, Tortula, Famaria, Trichostomum, Neckeræ, Polytrichum fuscum, Zygodon? Dendrobium and Otochilus, occur here. A stray and small Abies occurs on the ridge itself.

About the village of Bailfa occur Urtica urens, Artemisia major, Saccharum aristatum, Rubus triphyllus, Senecio scandens, Rumex, Chickweed, Stemodia ruderailis, Lactucoidea murorum, Carduus, Phlomoides, Rubus deltoidifolies, Achyranthoid, densa.

January 30th.—Thermometer at 7 A. M. 40°. The houses here are roofed with split bamboos, and they are tied on by rattans, a precaution rendered necessary by the boisterous winds which prevail.

The place is very cold; the thermometer varying from 40° to 52°. mean temperature of the day 46°.

In the barley fields I noticed Fumariæ sp., Potentilla and Cynoglossum, Erythrina ascends to this! Pyrus Malus and Spiræa bella occur.

January 31*st*.—Our march this day commenced with an ascent of a ridge lying to the north-east of our halting place, this occupied us some time, and at last we reached a pagoda, visible from Bailfa, and which is nearly 1,000 feet above that place. Thence we descended about a hundred feet, through a well-wooded situation. Emerging thence at about the same elevation, we crossed barren bleak downs, the ravines being alone wooded, and hence the woods had that rounded, defined appearance, so remarkable in some parts of the Khasya hills.

Thence the descent was continued to Roongdong, the march is an easy one, about seven miles.

The first new plant that occurred was an Allium on rocks, but it had been dried up by the fires which had bared the surface of the hill of every thing, except the trees and stouter shrubs, capable of resisting its action.

Toward the pagoda, on the summit of the ridge, Pendulous lichens were abundant, Epiphytes were common, consisting chiefly of Orchideæ, with the 2 Gay Lussacias, Rhododendron punctata, Hymenopogon parasiticus, Orthodon, Tussilaginoid, Alnus occurred at 7,300 feet. The other vegetation continued.

At 7,400 feet, a new Quercus appeared, this, which has in its young state, leaves much like those of the Holly, and may therefore be called *Q. elicifolia!* Andropogon, Viburnum cærulium, Neckera, Bambusa microphylla, Fragaria, Potentilla, Conyza nivea, Scabiosa Spiræa decomposita, Gillenioides, Smilax ruscordeus, Hyperica of Moflong, Campanula, Swertia, Dipsacus.

At 7,500 feet, Epilobium, Rosa, Vaccinum cyaneum! Rhododendron coccineum, Tetranthera.

At 7,800 feet, Abies pendulifolia, Hemiphragma.

At the pagoda, and about it, Grimmia was found on rocks, with the usual pendulous Neckeræ, Q. elicifolia, Vibura, Hipericum.

Abies Brunoniana, a large solitary tree, with pendulous branches, Tetranthera, Laurineæ, Smilax gaultherifolia, Ilex, on the wooded side of the ridge. Ferns and mosses were abundant, Ilex! Daphne papyracea.

Eurya, Panax rhododendrifolia, Rhododendron arborea, minus et majus. The tree of Thumathaya* foliis ad apicem ramorum aggregatis,

* Page 32.

petiolis colorat., Celastrinea Euryifolia, Tetranthera another species without leaves. In the more moist places a small Urticeæ, Lonicera as before, on the exposed side stunted Q. elicifolia, Dipsacus, Gnaphalia, Vaccinium cyaneum, and Gramineæ, Hemiphragma, Potentilla, Campanula, Tussilaginoides. Long-tailed grey monkeys.

The ridge we crossed, runs up into a bleak ridge on which are houses, and which cannot be under 9,500 feet high, about the descent through the wood, which did not extend many hundred yards. I noticed Galium, Valeriana, Crawfurdia fasciculata, Sphæropteris Betula corylifolia, Hypericum, Spiræa gillenioides, Rubus cordifolius, Senecio scandens, Juncus effusoideus, in wet places, Rhododendron majus, coming into flower, (flower white) Cerastium bacciferum, arborea, canescens, Cissus, Rubus moluccanus, Elæagnus, Rubus potentillifolia, Plantago, Ligustrum, Berberis pinnata and asiatica, which last is generally coyered with lichens.

Xanthoxylum, Lilium giganteum ! Polytrichium fuscescens, Trichostomum anielangioides, Pohlia, on walls and rocks, Adoxa ! in wet places under banks, with a fleshy Urticea : about this was observed the brick-red and black bird.*

Along the naked ridge and on the downs, which had a most wintery appearance, and where it was bitterly cold, the Lycopodium of Surureem was found, also Vaccinum cyaneum, Gnaphalium, Pteris aquelina stunted, Hypericum of Moflong, Swertia stunted, Hemiphragma.

The defined woods are formed of oaks and stray Abies pendulifolia, Panax rhododendrifolia, Berberis asiatica, and B. pinnata.

Mespilus microphyllus, Rhododendron minus, and R. arborea, (Euphorbia, and Juncus on the swards.) Eurya, Gaultheria arborea, Stauntonia. From this ridge a village near Benka is visible, as well as a large stream, the Goomrea, and several villages. The one we now inhabit, being the best looking and occupying a deep valley, is surrounded with much terrace cultivation.

Descending still farther we left the downs, first coming into the scraggy woods of Oaks, Rhododendron, Quercus, chiefly Q. robur.

About here we met abundance of people going to Hazoo from Kampo ; they were accompanied with asses chiefly carrying burdens of one maund weight ; few goats ; one yak was seen of a black colour ; a low compact animal, much resembling, except in the absence of a hump, the bison : it was not a handsome specimen. We

* Centropus nigrorufus.

also passed a village to the left, containing about twenty houses, here a Nai gooroo, or person of rank, resides, and here I also got fruit bearing specimens of Abies pendula.

Noticed, as I descended, Pyrus, Cerasus, Magnoliacea, Gaultheria arborea and frutex, Pteris aquelina, Quercus sclerophylla of Bulphai, Viburnum cærulescens and angustifola. ! Rhododendron minus, Ilex! Aspid. nidus, Gordonia, Q. lanata, Woodwardia, Rubia albiflora, Gleichenia major, Pyrus indica. Then we came to a pretty temple built like a house, with a fine specimen of Cypress pendula, altitude of the place 7,000 feet. From this a fine view of Roondong is obtained.

Still descending a short distance came to another temple, with a dome of the ordinary form, and a large square terraced basement, and inscribed slabs in the recesses. Hence the ascent was very steep. Erythrinum, Buddlea! Indigofera! Spiræa bella, Artemisia major! Polygonum rheoides! Rubus deltoidens! Curculigo, Conaria nepalensis, Thalictrum majus! Asparagus, Jubrung! Oxalis corniculata, Clematis cana, Eurya ferruginea! Santalacea australas, Pyrus malus! Elæocarpus! Mæsa salicifolia. We then crossed a small torrent, and ascended about 100 feet to Roongdong; noticed Stemodia grandiflora! Spiræa bella, Conaria, Erythrium, Elæagnus spinosus, Salix? buds with velvet or woolly hairs, Martynia! Hedera! Citrus! Woodwardia.

The transitions of the flora were this day well shewn. The plants which indicated the greatest elevation are, Vaccinium, Abies Brunoniana, Saxifraga, or Adoxa, Q. ilecifolia, Rhododendron formosum, R. arboreum majus, Sphæropteris, Ilex, Eurya acuminata? Panax rhododendrofol., Berb. pinnata and B. asiatica, Mespilus, Microphylla, Juncus.

The occurrence of the Urticea at such elevation is curious, the proofs of the wonderful effects of humidity, and non-exposure were particularly shewn, between the exposed south face of the Bulphai mountain, and the north-east face which was wooded.

From scarcity of grass, horses were here seen to feed on boughs so high as to be obliged to stand on stones, to get at their food. They are likewise fed on maize and tares; the poultry is of a large brood. The cocks are atrociously noisy, two in particular had such lengthened, cracked or quavering voices, that they were quite a nuisance. We put up in the house of the Dumpa or head man. It is situated on the top of a stony, and a bitter cold place, exposed to the four winds of heaven. House very large, and our host a little man with great airs, and a red coat or wrapper of coarse English cloth, drinks intensely.

During our stay at this place he invited Pemberton and Blake to shoot pigeons; the poor man thought that they would not be able to hit them, on finding out his mistake, he put an end to the sport.

Atriplex is cultivated here, Mooreesa of Assam, Hempstee of the Booteas, though seeds are used as well as the leaves.

The loads of salt brought down by the Tibetans on asses are packed up neatly in coarse cloths, and weigh upwards of forty seers each.

BOOTAN.

Bulphai, 6,808 ft. o .—Erythrina, Cnicus, Crucifera.
[Q. lanata Sclerophylla.
Rhodod. minus, Daphne, Piper.

.—Hypericum, Swertia.

.—Gymnostomum.
.—Q. ilicifol.
.—Allium.
.—Vaccinum, Scabiosa, Campanula.
.—Andropogon, Polytrichum.
.—Spiræa.

About 8,000 ft. .— | Trichosanthes on rocks.
} Ilex, Abies Br. Daphne.
Gaultheria nov. .— | Ferns, Urticea, Smilax geal.

Long-tailed ape. .—Sphæropteris, Crawfurdia.
.—Rhododendron 2.
.—Saxifraga.

Barren grassy downs. Stunted Pteris aquilina. .—Polytrichum Trichost., Pohlia.
.—Marchantiacea.

Woods occupying ravines with rounded distinct outlines, Quercus, Abies pendul., Mespilus, Microphyllum Berberis 2. Panax, Rhododendif., Daphne papyra, Vaccinia, Rhododend. minus. .—Vaccinium cyaneum.
.—Abies.

Villages occur here with a good deal of cultivation. .—Ilex, Magnolia, Cerasus.
.—Cypressus pendula.

.—Magnolia.
.—Woodwardia, Ruta albiflora.

.—Buddleæ, Erythrina.
.—Conaria nepalensis, P. rheoides, Pyrus Malus, Artemisia major.

Roongdong, 6,000 ft. o .—Citrus, Pol. rheoides, Mæsa, salicifolia, Hedera.]

February 1*st*.—Our march commenced by descending gradually at first, then very rapidly to the Dimree nuddee: crossing this at the junction of two streams, we ascended a little and then kept along the side of the ridge forming the right bank of the nuddee, until we came over the Monass : thence proceeding about one and a half mile, we reached Tassgong or Benka which is situated on this river, and about 1,000 feet above it. This we crossed by a suspension bridge.

But little interesting botany occurred to-day: Chenopodium sp. occurs in fields at Roongdong. The terrace cultivation here had just yielded a crop of rice, and was now planted with wheat. Agriculture would appear to be at a low ebb, and if the country is populous, the people must be half-starved.

Water was abundant throughout the route: the Monass is a large stream, but not generally very deep, although from its rapidity it must discharge even at this season a great body of water. Composita penduliflora descends to the Dimree, the altitude of which is about 3,000 feet, so in fact did most of the plants found about Roongdong. Pyrus continues half-way, Rhododendron to the bottom. Hovenia at an altitude of 5,000 feet, Randia—as also Tetranthera oleosa, and a new Flemingia.

At 4,900 feet, *Jubrung* occurs.—Clematis, Cana, Luculiæ sp., Conyzoidea nivea, Kydia calycina, Mimosa arborea, began at 4,800 feet: Gaultheria, arborea, Gordonia, descend to the bottom : Crawfurdia speciosa, Oxyspora, Aspidium, Macrostomium, and Polypodioides, Saurauja hispida, Hypericum, Spiræa bella, Gillenioinis, Quercus, Rubus, and Viburnum cærulescens. A tree yielding lac, which had lately been cut, and Meliaceæ, Rhus triphyllum. Hence some snow was visible on a lofty ridge above our heads, at least 9,500 feet, the snow descending a considerable way down ravines. Of birds, Bulbuls and Bucco, were here observed.

At —— feet, Leguminosa arborea, Loranthus Scurrula, Kydia Wendlandia, Celtis, Osbeckia nepalensis, a Vitex, Grislea, Pteris aquilina, Indigofera! Acanthacea cærulea.

At —— feet, Triumfetta mollis, Composita arborea, Pterospermum, fructibus 10-valvibus, valvis lobatibus, Sem. alatis. Santalacea australasica, here a large shrub.

At the nullah, Fici sp., Saccharum Megala, Verbenacia? foliis apice craso lobatis. On the opposite side, Pinus longifolia, to within 200 feet of the nullah, Phlibochiton extensus! Solanum farinaceum! Achyranthes densa! a Plumbaginacea ,which is a Pæderioid Rubiacca, and

2 *g*.

another Ficus, Hastingsia, Bassia, Labiata Sudyensis, Grislea, very common, Emblica, Ficus obliquus were found along the road, after crossing the nullah. The ridge of the mountain was rocky, barren, covered chiefly with grasses, the Butea of Nurtung, Artemisia minor, Umbelliferæ, Desmodium vestilum, Kalanchœ, also occurred. At the few houses below our path. we saw plantains! and bamboos as well as mangoes! The terraces here are fronted with stones: Lemna occurred in water; Linaria on rocks; Conaria and a fleshy Euphorbia, this last, about villages.

The occurrence of plantains and mangoes here is curious, and a sure sign of mild climate, as Kalanchoe is of dryness; nothing could well exceed the barrenness of the road, from crossing Dumria to Benka.

Benka is a straggling place, built on a ridge overhanging the Monass, and on exceedingly rugged ground, the north face of the ridge being nearly equally steep; the southern face, contains about fifty houses, all of which are small and a few in ruins. The only large house is the Rajah's, which is said to be of Chinese construction.

This day the Rajah paid us a visit; a tent was pitched for his reception on the open ground before our house, consisting of a small silken pall, with two high silken parti-coloured kunnauts. He arrived about eleven, preceded and succeeded by followers amounting to less than a hundred. On reaching the ground, he was carried or shuffled off his horse and deposited in the tent amid most terrific screechings. He took an immense time to arrange for our admission. We found him seated on a shabby throne, with a head priest, a coarse looking man, on his right, on a less elevated seat. Brass cups, etc. were arranged before him. Our chairs occupied the left; a present of fruits, onions, etc., the floor. The meeting was friendly, and he promised us coolies in two days. He is a youngish man with a square face, and was well dressed.

After we had taken leave, he feasted his attendants and the spectators with salt-fish and rice. He departed about 2 P. M. The procession was as follows, both going and returning—

A large, black, shaggy dog led by a chain.

A drum and drummer; a gong with a melodious sound; a clarionet played by an old and accomplished musician, rivalling in its strains that beautiful instrument the bagpipe; a man bearing a wooden painted slab on a pole, on this was an inscription; a banner looking like a composition of rags; a white flaglet; fifteen matchlockmen; fifteen bowmen; the Dompa of Roongdong; five horses and one mule led.

The household; Natchees; guitar; sundries. Personal attendants, looking like yeomen of the guard in red cloth dresses, variegated with yellow; the Rajah wearing a chinese copper hat.

Lastly, the priests, of whom there were about six.

These were the best clothed and best mounted, and evinced satisfactory tokens of being corporeally well off. Their dress consisted of a sombre jacket with no sleeves, with either a yellow or red silk back, over this is a sombre scarf. They are great beggars, and the headman was well pleased with a present of four rupees. In return, he gave P. two, B. and myself each one paper of salt, similar to those given to the lookers-on.

The ponies were all poor, excepting two or three of the Rajah's own, which were handsomely equipped; these had their tails raised on end, exactly like hobby-horses. In addition to this, each was supplied with supernumerary yâk tails, one on either side.

The whole people collected did not amount to more than 300. The arms, at least were wretched, consisted of culverins, which went off with an enormous report, and matchlocks with short rests, like the end of a pitchfork. The bows were long and good. The helmets were worn on the head when going and coming, but were allowed to sling on the back while resting here; they are rude iron things, like bowls, but covered for some way up the sides with cloth in a most unbecoming way. Dirt and noise were predominant; the dancing women, evidently not what they should be, had clean faces, but horridly dirty feet, and were very plain. The dancing was poor, consisting chiefly of ungraceful motions of the hands and forearms; the singing pleasing, harmonious but monotonous.

A peculiar kind of spirit called *Chonghoons* is in great requisition: this liquor is pleasant, perfectly clear like whiskey and water, with a small matter of malt in it.

Fumaria is found here much more advanced than that at Bulphai, Drymaria ovata. They cultivate one sort of Legume, perhaps more; mangoes, jacks and pomegranates; all these trees bear fruit towards the end of the hot weather. A young mango tree was observed with opposite leaves, uppermost pair one abortive nearly: thus the Mariam of Burma, may probably present the normal form of foliation. *Adoee* fish* found in the Monass.

Bheirs, papia, tobacco, banyan, of these last, poor specimens may be seen here. The place is miserably poor, and as it is reckoned one of

* *Oreinus progastus*, As. Res. vol. xix. pl. 40, fig. 4.

some importance, its condition shows the barrenness of the oountry. The Rajah's house is a large one, apparently consisting of a quadrangle with an elevated story. News arrived yesterday to the effect that tumults still prevailed: the Deb it was said had been deposed by treachery: that a new one had been permanently appointed: but that the usurper did not wish us to come on. Tongsa, however, said that after we have come so far, we should advance, and that we may settle our plans at his place.

February 5th.—Left: descended immediately from the town to the bridge over the Monass. The descent is steep but winding, the face of the hill being nearly precipitous. Close to the river we passed a small field of Cajanus, used for feeding the lac insect. The bridge is a suspension one, the chains, one on either side, being of iron in square links the curve is considerable, in the form of the letter V, the sides being of mat. Hence it is difficult to cross, and this is increased by the bridge swinging about considerably: it is seventy yards in span, and about thirty above the Monass.

The Monass is 1,300 feet below Benka, it is a large river, the banks being about eighty yards apart, but this space is not generally filled with water. Its violence is extreme.

We continued along this river some time, gradually rising from its bed until we ascended nearly 1,000 feet. We continued at this elevation until we reached Nulka, to which place we descended a little. The whole march was through a barren, rocky, burnt up country. The Monass was in sight nearly the whole distance. Passed two villages, both small, one on the right and one on the left bank of the river. No change in vegetation occurred except that we came upon pines, P. longifolia about a mile and a half from Nulka, coming into flower. I am almost inclined to think this is different from the Khasya species, Kurrimia, Indigofera pulchra, Desmodium, Buddleia sp., were the only plants of a novel nature that occurred. The hills are chiefly clothed with Andropogoneous grasses, very little cultivation was observed, but there seemed to be more on high hills to the east.

Bheir, jack, pomegranate, mango, banyan, Santalaceæ, Jasminum.
Ficus, tobacco, papia, Euphorbia, Solanum farinaceum.
Stemodia secunda, Hastingsia, Pæderia fœtida, and P. cyaneceum.
} Tassgong 3,182 feet.

Rhus pendula, Grislea, Kalanchoe.
Artemisia minor, Andropogonous grasses, Deeringia.
Vitex negundo.

Cajanus, mango.

Monass river, or Goongree 1,400 feet above the sea.

Emblica, Pterospermum. —Bauhinia, Mimosa, Arundo, Rottlera.

—Kurrimia, Ficus oblique.

Andropogoneous grasses, Arioides, all burnt up, Kalanchoe. —Indigofera, Cassia fistula.

—Pinus longifolia.

—Lactuca hastata.

—Buddlæa.
—B. neemda.

—Vitex negundo.

Pomegranate, plantain, China rose, sugarcane. Rice cultivation along the Monass, which is 800 feet below this place. —Nulka 2,200 feet.

CHAPTER XII.

Continuation of the journey in Bootan.

The following table affords the result of observations made with the view to determine the relation between temperature and altitude, in these parts.

	Difference of Temperature.	Difference of Elevation.	Value in height of 1° of Temperature.
Benka and Monass,....	13° Fahr.	1,222 feet.	94 feet.
,, and Nulka,......	4 =	406 =	$101\frac{5}{10}$
,, and Khumna,...	13 =	1,110 =	85-5
Khumna and Nulka,.. ...	16 =	1,516 =	89-3
Monass and Nulka,.....	9 =	816 =	90-6
Monass and Khumna,...	26 =	2,332 =	89-9
			6)550-8

Mean value of 1° of Fahr. as indicated on the barometer. 91-8

Second series of observation.

Benka and Monass,....	13° Fahr.	1,193-4 feet	91-8 feet
,, Nulka,.....	4 =	367-2 =	91.8
,, Khumna,...	13 =	1,178-1 =	90-6
Khumna and Nulka,....	17 =	1,557.0 =	91-10
Monass and Nulka,....	9 =	826-2 =	91-8
,, and Khumna,..	26 =	2,386-8 =	91-8
			6)549-8
			91-6

The Monass is called Goongree by the Booteas; its bed is very much inclined, and tranquil pools are of rare occurrence: it is not fordable in any place, although many of the rapids are not very deep. The singular bridge is said to be of Chinese construction, and that it serves the purpose of a chief thoroughfare, is a proof of the extremely small population of the country.

Onions grow at Nulka, plantains, sugarcane, tobacco.

Bheirs are common. Weeping cypress occurs, but stunted.

The entrance to this village on the north-side, is through a square building, the ceiling of which is painted, and the walls decorated with figures of deities, white and red.

From a Sketch made on the spot by W. Griffith.

KOLLONG BRIDGE

M & N Hanhart, lith Printers

February 6th.—We descended immediately to the Monass, keeping along its banks throughout the greater part of the march; rising however, over one or two spurs that dip into it.

This river varies a good deal in width, its bed, however, is generally confined, and the stream fierce; occasionally, however it spreads out and becomes here and there more placid. We continued along its banks, crossing one or two small streams until 12 o'clock, when we reached a large torrent, the Koollong, up which we proceeded three or four hundred yards, but at some height above its bed. We crossed this by a wooden bridge of similar construction with that over the Deo Panee, and the idea of which is ingenious. It is nearly fifty yards wide, and about twenty above the torrent. It is in a bad state, and unprovided with railings throughout the central level part. The houses into which the inclined supporting beams are fixed are strong, and built on rock. The fastenings are altogether of cane, and the whole presenting the appearance given in the annexed drawing.

Hence we ascended a black, rocky, burnt up mountain until we reached Khumna, the ascent amounted to nearly 2,000 feet, and occupied more than an hour.

But little of interest occurred, in fact I never saw a more barren country. We passed a small village of two or three houses, and two good patches of rice cultivation, one just below Nulka, one at Ghoomkhume, the small village just alluded to.

Pinus longifolia descends nearly to the bed of the Monass, which below Nulka is about 2,200 feet above the level of the sea. Along this I noticed Hiræa, Eugenia, Vitis, Jasminum, Pæderia fœtida, Ficus, Loranthus, Scurrula, Desmodium, Aerides, Vanda, Flacourtia, Kalanchoe, Leguminosa, *Vanillidora* of *Solani mookh*, Ceanothus, Bergera, Dischidia bengalensis, Leguminous trees, Euphorbia, Bassia, Cheilanthes of Brahmakoond common, Coccoloba cyanea. In rice khets at Ghoomkurrah, I found Lemna, Cardamine, Rumex of Khejumpa, Cirsium decurrens, Gnaphalia, Datura, Simool in flowers; Spathoidea, Oxalis coriculata, Cannabis, Verbesina.

I observed water-ouzels, bucco, water-wagtails, bulbuls, ordinary and yellow-rumped.

BOOTAN.

Nulka 2,200 feet. —Sugarcane, Bheir, tobacco, onions.

—Bhobosa, maize, rice Buddlæa.

—Indigofera, Santalacea, Desmodium.

—Flacourtia, Pinus.

—Bauhinia, Dischidia bengalensis, Ficus, Pterosperma.

—Leguminous trees, Hiræa, Saccolabium.

— Simool, Flemingia secunda. Gnaphalium, Rumex.

—Cirsium decurrens.

All the features tropical. Pines not within 300 feet; grasses, etc. as before, about Benka.

Koollong bridge. Monass and Koollong rivers join at this point.

—Ixora, Euphorbia.

Bleak, rocky, burnt up hills, without a blade of grass.

Khumna 4,292 feet. —Pinus longifola.

Passed cotton cultivation in two places, one close to the Monass, and one to the Koollong, both equally bad, and observed Begonia edule, which they call Sheemptsee, and which they eat.

The road to-day was generally good, overhanging in one place the Monass at a height of forty yards above, and below scarped precipices. The road here was constructed or supported artificially. Distance six miles.

February 7th.—To Phoollong. Left at 9½ A. M., and immediately commenced ascending. The ascent was at first steep, then gradually wound round the Khumna mountain, which was most barren throughout. The ascent continued but very gradually until we came near Phoollong, to which we descended, and then ascended about 100 feet. About half-way, and when we had ascended perhaps 1,000 feet, we came on new vegetation, oaks, Rhododendra, etc. as before, and this continued improving in denseness until we reached the village. The distance is five miles, ascent about 1,500 feet, but so gradual, that one would not imagine it more than 800 feet. At Khumna, I noticed Pinus longifolia, Pyrus malus, Achyranthes dense, Citrus, Urtica urens, tobacco, Musa, Datura, Artemisia major. Hogs are fed here in large circular platters made of stone scooped out

Commencing the ascent, I observed Ficus cordata of Bhamru, Rhus pendula, Indigofera *elatior*, Conaria, Pteris aquilina, Cerasus commenced at 5,000 feet. Then Desmodium vestilum, Artemisia minor, Conyza laculia, Rubus deltifolius, Labiata Sudyensis, Acanth. cærulescens.

Quercus robur commenced at about 5,200 feet, but stunted. Flemingia secunda, then Gaultheria arborea, Gnaphalium nivea.

Here there was a high ridge to the right, crowned with a wood of Q. robur, all the leaves of which had fallen. Myrica, Rhododendron, Jubrung, Didymocarpus contortus on rocks, Cnicus, Clematus cana, Polygonum rheoides. At a village here, which contained ten houses, observed Cupressus pendula, Citrus, wheat, Bambusa, then Juncus. Primula of the Khasya hills. Q. robur abundant, Composita penduliflora, Saurauja hispida, Equisetum, Rubus cæsius, Alnus of Thumathaya, Elæagnus spinosus, E. macrophyllus 5,300 feet: Plantago, Coriaria, Erythrina, Rhus acidum, Cerastium cœnum, Dipsacus, Viburnum microphyllum, Rubia cordifolia, Barleria, Tetranthera oleosa, Hedera, Gentiana, Myrsine, Blasia, Fleshy urticea, Q. robur, Gordonia, Adamia, Neckera jungermannoides and læta, Primula in abundance, Acorus, Calamus, Scirpus kysoor of Churra, Gram. latifolia, Andropogonoides of Suniassa.

2 *h*

Coming on a well-wooded ravine close to Phoollong, the first I have seen since leaving Balphai, found Quercus 2, Castanea, Gordonia, Spiræa decomposita, and S. Bella, Hydrangia, Rhododendron, Thalictrum, Quercus, Curculigo, Viburnum cærulescens, Indigofera elatior, Gnaphalium niveum, Sempervivum on rocks, Panicum eleusinoides, Thibaudia myrtifolia, Swertia major, Alnus as before, Rubus moluccanus, Salix lanata, Primula Simsii, Phlomoides, Orthodon.

Throughout the march we observed many detached houses on the mountains forming the right bank of the Koollong, and much cultivation, all of the terrace sort. Passed one village beneath us about 700 feet, containing, twelve houses, and the one mentioned above; as usual, ruined houses occur.

Cattle furnished with litters of leaves; a curious low was heard, like that of an elephant.

Booteas work their own cotton, much of which is cultivated along the rivers at low elevations.

Higher land, certainly 11 to 12,000 feet high, was visible to the north side: on this a good deal of snow was visible.

KHUMNA TO PHOOLLONG.

Khumna, 4,292 feet. — Citrus, Pinus longifolia. Sugarcane, Urtica urens

Barren, rocky, bleak, burnt up hill. —Andropogonous grasses, Artemisia minor. —Conyza, Rhus pendula, Ficus.

At this point the vegetation commences to change. —Quercus robur. —Rhododendron, stunted Pines.

Chalee, 5,200 feet. — Citrus, Bambusa, Cupressus pendula.

—Primula.

Viburnum microphyllum. —Quercus robur, Gordonia. —Primula, Neckera jungermannoides. —Acorus, Juncus.

Hills all more or less wooded, ridges covered with woods of Q. robur. *Jay* as before.

—Quercus, Castaneæ, Spiræa. —Hydrangea, Thalictrum. —Primula.

—Sempervivum. —Fleshy urticeæ, Primula.

Lofty range overtopping this, 8,500 feet, on which there is snow.

— Phoollong about 6,000 feet.

February 8th.—Towards the morning it commenced to rain; snow has fallen on both sides the Koollong: it has fallen on the road we came by yesterday, and on the hills above to within 200 feet of us, or in some places to the level of this. Exemption in favour of this place is to be attributed to local causes. The trees in the neighbourhood are completely covered with it, and it is said to have fallen here twice during the night.

The Bootea houses are ill calculated for rain, they leak all around as indeed might be expected from the nature of the roofs, which consist of boards, kept *in situ* by stones. It would be curious to ascertain the temperature under which snow does not fall, and if possible the temperature here and among the snow. In the morning, sleet with a few flakes of snow fell also, but only occasionally.

Snow continued to fall throughout the day, and steadily too: it commenced slightly: as the cold increased it ceased to melt on reaching the ground, and at length all around was a sheet of white. The variations of the thermometer were considerable and frequent, the wind blowing pretty steadily from the south-east.

At	10	A. M.	37	degrees	Snow commencing.
,,	$10\frac{1}{2}$	,,	36	,,	South-east wind.
,,	$10\frac{3}{4}$	,,	40	,,	Wind from the north, snow rather heavy.
,,	$11\frac{3}{4}$	,,	37	,,	South-east.
,,	12	,,	35	,,	ditto.
,,	$12\frac{1}{2}$	,,	36	,,	ditto.
,,	$2\frac{1}{2}$	,,	37	,,	ditto.
,,	4	,,	39	,,	ditto.
,,	6	,,	37	,,	ditto.
,,	9	,,	38	,,	ditto.

Fine moonlight night. View to the north beautiful; every thing silvered with snow; the deep and black ravine of the Koollong is particularly conspicuous, and on some cultivated spots the pendulous cypress with its sombre head and branches covered with snow, was also remarkable, altogether a beautiful scene. Larch-like firs were visible 500 feet over the road leading to this from Khumna.

February 9th.—Fine sunny morning: thermometer at 7 A. M. 35°: at 8 A. M. 42°. Hills around covered with snow. High ridge to south plainly visible, a good deal of snow visible. Went out at noon over to the south-east, in which direction a pine wood was visible; this I ascertained to consist of Pinus or Abies pendula, which has much the habit of a Larch. The altitude of this above Phoollong is certainly 1,000 feet; snow covered the ground in all sheltered spots. The woods here are formed chiefly of Q. robur, Q. elecifolia also occurs here and there, Gordonia, Cerasus, Rhododendron minus.

Mosses and Jungermanniæ abound, and were in high perfection owing to being saturated with moisture. Polytrichum, Neckera, Brachymenium, Dicranum, Weissiæ, Fissidens, Hypnum, Didymodon, Diastoma, Orthodon, were found in perfection. The only new plant were a Campanula and a Chimaphila, which last was found at 7,000 feet. Berberis asiatica scarcely occurs below 6,000 feet, Hedera. The birds seen were the jay, barbet, red-and-black-headed, variegated short-wing, large ditto of Khegumpa, orange-breasted Trochilus, brown Fringilla, green woodpecker, black pheasant, and small squirrel of Assam was also found.

From the fir wood, Tassyassee was distinctly visible, bearing nearly due south, distance 10 or 12 miles. Koollong was also seen: all the high ground between that and Bulphai was covered with snow. The high range to the south is, I think, the same as that which runs up behind from the pagoda above Bulphai.

A few plants of the Assam Indigo, Ruellia indigofera, are kept here, and preserved with care, but stunted and obviously unsuited to the climate. Montario, our taxidermist, says that it is the fourth plant he knows from which indigo is procured. First, Indigofera —Second, the custard-apple, *shereefa*—Third, a climbing plant used in Java, etc. probably Marsdenia tinctoria—Fourth,— ?

February 10*th.*—Fine weather: thermometer at 7 A. M. 40° Started at 9 A. M., and reached Tassyassee at 3 P. M.; the distance being nine miles. We continued throughout nearly at the same elevation, rounding the hill on which Koollong is placed. About three miles from this we descended about 500 feet to a nullah, which we crossed over by means of planks, thence we ascended about the same height, and continued at nearly our former level until we descended to the Koollong, which we crossed by the usual form of wooden bridge. Thence we ascended 400 feet to the village, which is chiefly constituted by the Rajah's house, a very large edifice. The Koollong is still a considerable stream, but appears to be fordable, at least in the present season.

The vegetation continued the same almost throughout. In ascending from the nullah above mentioned, we came on plenty of Pinus longifolia, and on getting still nearer Tassyassee the Abies pendula became more and more common, until it forms on the opposite bank of the Koollong opposite this, a large wood; Pinus longifolia disappearing. The hills continue openly wooded, the woods consisting of oaks, chiefly Q. robur and Rhododendrons. In the ravines which are thickly wooded, oaks, chesnuts, Cerasus, Rhododendron arborea, mosses; Panax two or three species, among which is a new one, *P. æsculifolia*, arbor parva armati, foliis 7 digittatis, paniculis nutantibus. Hydrangea, Viburnum cærulescens, and Microphyllum, Galium, Ferns abundant, Bucklundia likewise occurred here and there! Tetranthera, Valeriana, Scabiosa, Conaria, Holcus elegans.

In the broken ground before reaching this, Gaultheria nummularifolia, Primula minor, in crevices of rocks. In some places Erythrina was very common, Gentiana, Dipsacus, Sedum and Didymocarpus contortus on rocks, Saccharum aristatum, Salix lanata, Woodwardia, Primula minor, which grows in shade on the Khasya hills, is found here in sunny wet places. The scenery in some places is very romantic, and occasionally grand; the valley of the Koollong being closed far to the north by a high ridge and beautiful peaks, all heavily snowed. The Rajah's house is visible from a considerable distance. As we approached, some parts were rugged and bold. Water abundant throughout.

Phoollong 5,929 feet.	
Wheat, Bhobosa, Cupressus pendula, Room.	Solanum melongena, Thlaspi arista.
	Ervum, Crucifera, Ajuga.
Oak woods; chiefly Q. robur.	
Oak woods with Rhododendrons.	
Usual Andropogoneous grasses.	
	Conaria.
Tetranthera, Viburn. cærulescens and microphyllum.	Valeriana, Scabiosa, Galium.
	Hydrangea, Castanea, Quercus.
	Holcus elegans, Galium.
	Erythrina, Artemisia major.
Hooked-tailed Finch, large, short-wing.	
Orange-breasted Trochilus.	Alnus.
Didymocarpus contortus.	Bucklandia, Rhodod. arbor. maj
Sedum, Sempervivum.	Panax æsculifolium.
	Orthodon, Orthotrichum, Gricemia.
Thalictrum majus.	Primula minor, Spiræa decomposita, Gilleneoides.
	Fleshy urticæ, Woodwardia, Begonia !
	Panax palmata.
	Primula Stuartii, Pinus longifolia.
	Alnus.
Lycopodium pendulum.	Pinus longifolia, with Abies pendula.
	Saccharum aristatum, Salix lanata.
Green Pigeon.	Gaultheria nummularifolia.
	Primula Stuartii.
Hypna, Funaria.	Abies pendula in woods, Composita pendulifora.
Koollong river.	
	Tassangsee 5,387 feet.

February 11*th*.—Went out at 1 P. M.; descending to, and crossed the Koollong, then ascending along its banks for about a mile.

The bridge over this is about thirty yards wide, abutting from two houses of ordinary structure, built on solid rocks: the river is underneath the bridge apparently of great depth; above it is a succession of rapids, it is even at this, the dryest season, a considerable river. The path leads in a winding direction either over rice cultivation or on precipitous banks. I noticed Berberis asiatica, pinnata, a Pomacea spinosa, foliis spathulatis, Stauntonia latifolia, Hedera, Gaultheria two or three, Thebandiaceæ, Artemisia major, Erythrina, Primula Stuartii in abundance, Juncus, Alnus, Myrsina, Prunella in grassy spots, Rumex of Khegumpa, Daphne papyracæ, Peperomia quadrifolium, Spiræa bella, Viola, Ophiopogon linearifol., Hypericum, Smilax, Elæagnus, Conaria, Lonicera villosa, Epilobium sericeum, a common plant in all watery places, Cardamina Swertia, Viburnum microphyllum. Rhododendrum arborea and minor, Leucas ciliata, Thistles, Pteris aquilina, Neckeræ, Osbeckia capitata of Churra, Oaks, Catharinea, Xyris, Gordonia, Fragaria, Potentilla two, Festucoidea, Cupressus pendula.

The greatest acquisitions were a beautiful pink farinaceous ascapous Primula, and a new genus of Hamamelideæ. This plant I have long known, and called *Betula corylifolia*, as I had only seen it in fruit, and not examined it; it is found on the Khassya hills at elevations of between 4,000 and 6,000 feet. It will be worth dedicating it to some distinguished geologist, thereby associating his name with that of Bucklandia and Sedgwickii.

No fly-fishing is to be had in this stream, nor indeed in any at such elevations. The Adoee is found, but always keeps at the bottom, the structure of its mouth pointing out its grovelling habits. The Bookhar does not, I think, ascend more than 2,500 feet. Water-ouzels, white-fronted Sylvia occur. Observed for the first time the religious vertical revolving cylinders, these revolve by the action of water, which runs on the cogs of the wheel by means of hollowed out trunks of trees. Flour mills are common here, the grindstone revolves on another by means of vertical spokes, which are set in motion by a horizontal wheel, and moved by a stream let on it in the same way.

Funaria heygrometrina abounds in the larch wood here.

This is a very cold place, although 550 feet below Phoollong: it is much colder than that place: thermometer at 7 A. M. 34°.

Snow still remains on the height around; heavy snow on the lofty ridge to the north: strong south-east winds prevail here.

From a sketch made on the spot by W. Griffith.

TASS-GOUNG FROM THE KOLLONG

M & N Hanhart, Lith Printers.

February 12*th.*—Tassyassy, which is also called Tassangsee, is a small place apparently consisting of one large house, belonging to the Soobah, and some religious edifices, the other houses belonging to it are scattered about among the adjoining cultivation. The Soobah we have just learnt is absent at Tongsa, so we have no opportunity of comparing his rank with that of the Tassgong man. His house is however, much larger; it is situated on a promontory formed by the debouching of a considerable sized torrent into the Koollong. The bridge is at the foot of this hill, which is about 400 feet high: the house is accessible to the north and west only. Half-way up a high hill to the north-west is a fort! and between the foot of this hill and the Rajah's house there is a wall with a tower at the north-west end, and a house at the south-east. In the afternoon the weather threatened snow, but it ended in very slight rain.

February 13*th.*—Thermometer at 7 A. M. 33°: at 9 P. M. 31°: cloudy. Observed Conyza nivea, Composita penduliflora, Agrimonia, Stemodia grandiflora, a species of Alopecurus in inundated rice fields, Fragaria, in the wood, Arenaria, Gymnostomum on the terraces. An Arabis in cornfields with a Viola, probably V. patrinia, Gaultheria deflexa and Gerardia of Churra. The fir woods are comparatively bare of mosses and lichens. Shot an Alauda, a Fringilla, and a curious climber with the tail of a woodpecker, at least so far as regards the pointing of the feathers, plumage of Yunx, and beak of Certhia.

Fine cypresses were seen opposite Tassangsee.

February 14*th.*—Left Tassangsee, diverging from the Koollong at that place, and following the nullah, which falls into that river below the Soobah's house. The march was a generally, continued, gradual ascent; we crossed two considerable streams by means of rude wooden bridges, and the whole march was a wet splashy one, owing to the abundance of water. Snow became plentiful towards the latter end. The direction was west, the distance about seven miles. We passed two or three deserted villages.

We commenced ascending through woods of stunted oaks, Rhododendrons, Gaultheria arborea. The chief under-shrubs being Daphne papyracæ, Gaultheria fruticosa, Primula Stuartii, Lycopodium of Surureem, Thibaudia myrtifolia continue, the Alnus of Beesa occurred plentifully along the bed of the nullah. Spiræa decomposita, Valeriana simplicifolia, Conaria, Scabiosa, Fragaria, Potentilla, Geranium, Artemisia major, Spiræa bella, Hedera, Viburnum cærulescens, Q. robur, Crawfurdia speciosa also occurred.

2 *i*

Ascending, the oaks and Rhododendrons became more developed the latter being the smaller species, Bambusa microphylla, Gordonia, Sphœropteris, Antrophyum trichomanes, Oxalis major ! commenced. Larches on the opposite side, Saccharum aristatum, Gillenioides, Gleichenia major, Hemiphragma, Abies Brunonis commence.

At 6,500 feet Smilax ruscoides, Senecio scandens, Lilium giganteum. The Rhododendrons here are large, forming with oaks, open woods, mosses and lichens, very abundant. Here we came on snow, with it commenced Eurya acuminata, Rhododendron formosa, majus, Rhododendron fruticosa on ruins, Pyrus malus, Dipsacus.

At 6,800 feet, Q. ilecifolia, Q. glauca, Dalibarda, Bambusa very common, Sphagnum abundant, Rhododendron formosa, majus, Quercus ilecifolia larger and more common at 7,000 feet, Gaultheria nummulariodes very abundant, Daltonia, Lomaria of Khegumpa, Gaultheria flexuosa, Thibaudia acida, Tetranthera nuda, Lycopodium of Surureem, Primula Stuartii, Hyperici sp., also *H. moflongensis*, are found up to 7,400 feet, with Hemiphragma, Elæagnus spinosus, microphyllum, Juncus, Alnus of Beesa, Saccharum aristatum.

The village is a ruined one apparently, and never contained more than four or five houses, situated on an open spot, surrounded by woods. This spot is covered with sward, a fine Q. ilecifolia occurs about the centre of the village. Its altitude is 7,983 feet.

The vegetation is the same, Abies pendula, Oaks, Rhododendron formosa, majus, the other has disappeared, Bambusa microphylla, Thibaudia acida, Primula Stuartii, Juncus.

TASSANGSEE TO SANAH.

Tassangsee 5,387 feet. Gneiss and mica slate.	—Cupressus, the pendula, larger. Trogon with small wing.
	—Spiræa decomp. Primula Stuartii, Hamamelis
	—Alnus.
	—Scabiosa, Valeriana, Rhododron. Daphne papyracæ, Conaria, Geranium, Potentilla.
	—Fragaria, Spiræa bella, Crawfurdia speciosa
	—Villarsia fragilis.
At 6,000 feet, Bamb. microphyllus,	—Gleichenia major, Gordonia.
Oxalis, Antrophyrum.	—Sphæropteris, Rhododendron. oaks.
At 6,500 feet, Hedera.	—Abies pendula, Brunonis, Gillonia.
	—Smilax ruscoideus, Lilium giganteum
	—Pyrus.
At 6,800 feet, Bambusa microphyllus.	—Rhod. formosa, majus, Q. ilecifolia.
Tetranthera nuda.	—Sphagnum, Dalibarda, Daltonia.
Lycopodium of Sursureem.	—Lomaria of Khegumpa.
Hypericum, H. mollongensis, Elæagnus. Saccharum aristatum, Alnus.	—Q. glauca, ilecifolia, Gaultheria flexuosa.
Juncus	—Primula Stuartii.
Sanah 7,983 feet. Mica slate.	

February 15th.—We started very early; the coolies were all off by 6½ A. M. Our march was first over undulating ground, either sward or through green lanes. We then commenced ascending a steep hill visible from Sanah, the face of which was covered with sward; at the top of this, snow lay rather thick, especially in the woods. The ascent continued, soon becoming very steep, snow laying heavily on the path, until we reached the summit of the second ridge; thence we descended a little, soon ascending again very steeply until we surmounted the highest ridge. The descent from this was at first most steep, the path running in zig-zags, and being in many places very difficult. About 1,000 feet below, we came on sward, with wood on the right, along which we descended, diverging subsequently through a thick wood, until we reached sward again. Here the coolies who had come up had halted, refusing to go on, as it was already dusk. Learning that Pemberton and B. had gone on, I hurried on likewise, expecting that the coolies would follow, and continued along the swardy ridge, the path running occasionally between patches of wood, the descent being gradual; the path then struck off into wood, and the descent became rapid. I continued onward, until it was quite dark, and finding it impossible to proceed, and meeting with no signs of B. and P., I determined on returning. I reached the coolies about eight, covered with mud, the path in the wood being very difficult and excessively slippery. I had nothing but broken crusts to eat; I procured some sherry however, and my bedding being up, I was glad to take shelter for the night under the trees. Next morning on overtaking P. and B., I found that they had remained all night in the wood without any thing to eat, and without bedding, and that no habitation was near. We reached the village about 9½ on the 16th, fatigued and dispirited. Nothing was at hand, and we had no meal until 5 P. M. except some tea, and an egg or two.

Many of the coolies came up late on the 16th, and some have not yet arrived (17th.) The distance was fifteen miles, to the halting place about twelve. The amount of ascent about 4,500 feet, and descent 6,100 feet, the road being difficult and very slippery: snow was heavy throughout, and the elevations between 9 and 12,400 feet; icicles were frequent. The trees were all covered with frost, and the aspect was wintry in the extreme; luckily there was no wind, and no snow fell. The summit of the ridge was 12,477 feet high. No views were obtained throughout the 15th and 16th; the weather being cloudy and very disagreeable. No bad effects were experienced from the rarefaction of the air; we all suffered of course from colds owing to exposure at night, at an elevation of nearly 9,500 feet; the servants bore it tolerably well.

At Sanah, the altitude of which is 7,983 feet, (Pemb.) I observed Quercus ilecifolia, on it Neckeræ, Antymenium, Senecio scandens, Rhododendron arboreum, majus, Juncus effusus, Swertia, Pendulous lichens, Dipsacus, Artemisia major, Primula Stuartii, Berberis asiatica, Bambusa microphylla, Lycopodium of Surureem, Orthotrichum!

At 8,000 feet, Smilax ruscoideus, Senecio scandens, woods of oak and Rhododendrons, the ground and the trees covered with mosses. Gnaphalium, Daphne papyrif., Mespilus microphyllus! Gaultheria nummularioides, Spiræa gillenioides, and S. bella, Hypericum, Gnaphalium lanceolatum, trivenum, Sambucus! but withered, Tetranthera nuda of Bulphai, Abies Brunonis which is probably a Podocarpus.

At 8,300 feet, Tussilaginoides of Churra, Primula Stuartii common on swards with Swertiæ, etc. as before, Funaria and Weissia Templetonia common, Sphæropterus! Quercus ilecifolia, Abies pendula, Rhododendron arboreum, majus! Dalibarda, Rubus, Ilex dipyrena! Rhododendron undulatum!

At 8,400 feet, the road running along, and above a ravine, rocky ground to the right, Eurya acuminata! Composita penduliflora. Thibaudia rotundifolia, and in a swampy sward a small dwarfed very narrow leaved bamboo, Primula Stuartii, Gnaphalium densiflorum, Swertia monocotyledonea, Prunella in the woods, Salix lanata, and Panax rhododendrifolia.

Just above this, 8,500 feet, the first Abies cedroides appeared, soon becoming very common, and extending up to 9,500 feet, its habit is like that of a cedar, and it is a tall handsome tree, Rubia* cordifolia! Geranium scandens, Baptisioides.

Crossing a nullah, we commenced a steep ascent, Thibaudacæ rotundifolia, Abies cedroides, Lomaria of Khegumpa, Crawfurdia speciosa, Andropogon, Gaultheria nummulacifol. Ilex, Epibolium Vaccinum cyaneum! Here a sward commenced with vegetation as before, the summit of this ascent was 9,050 feet. Here Ilex, Daphne papyracæ, Rhododendron, Scleria, Lomaria of Khegumpa! Primula pulcherrima! Spiræa bella, Gnaphalium trivenium, Rubus moluccanus, Thibaudia, Ericinea orbiculens, Spiræa decomposita, Gaultheria, nummulariod., Scutellaria prunella, Gaultheria flexuosa, Scandent composita, Cerastium bacciferum. The trees covered with mosses,

Neckeræ, Dicranum, Daltoniæ, Abies pendula ceased, its limits visible below. Hence the ascent was gradual at first: snow became heavy at 9,100 feet. Hemiphragma, Rhododendron abundant.

At 9,500 feet, much the same vegetation, Abies densa commenced, cedroides ceased. Woods entirely of A. densa, with a small baccatelike deciduous leaved tree. Hydrangea ! Spiræacea ! Urticeæ ?! Pedicularis elatior.

At 10,000 feet, some trees all covered with frost; snow very heavy, quite crisp. Juncus niveus, Cerastium inflatum ! bamboos, other plants of 9,500 feet, continue. Old Cretins !

At 11,270 feet, thermometer 39°, the same trees, scarcely any thing but Abies, Arenoid, Dicranum macrocarpus, Orthotrichum, Lichen pendulum atratum.

Thence we descended a little, soon to re-ascend.

At the same elevation Parnassia, Epilobium monus, Gnaphalium densiflor., Vaccinum pumilum, Gentiana, Polygonum (?)

At 11,000 feet, icicles were common, and snow very heavy. Woods of some Abies, a species of rose very abundant, a shrub of four feet high; other plants continue as before.

From this to the summit the ascent was very steep; Abies continues. Rhododendron (?) very common, with rose, Parnassia, Saxifraga, Composita arenoid, Gentiana, Polygonum (?), Pedicularis dwarfed, Triticoides, Aroides. Many pines dead as if blasted. Summit nearly bare of trees, which appear confined to slopes, Rhododendron very common, Umbellifera crassa, figured in Royle, Lilium unifloria.

At 12,000 feet, after descent, commenced Hymenophyllum, Xyris on rocks, Pyrus at 11,500 feet, Rhododendron ellipticum common, summit strewed with rocks, Rhododendron pumilum.

At 10,000 feet, the Spilus microphyllus, Polygonum, as well as on ascent Gaultheria nummularioid., swards abounding with Gramen nardoides (?), Dipsacus minor, Epilobium parnassia, Swertia, Umbelliferæ, Primula scapigerc. floribus in globum densum, pedalis, Habenariæ herminioid.

At the halting place 9,700 feet, Berberis ilecifolia, Daphne papyracæ, Thibaudia myrtifolia, Baptisia, Dipsacus, major, Swertiæ pedicularis, Andropogones, Ilex dipyrena, Rumex of Khegumpa, Betula, Euonymus cornutus, Abies cedroides, and Brunonis, Geranium scandens, Pyrus, Hypericum moflongensis, Hemiphragma, Mespilus microphyllus, Panax rhododendrifol., Rhododendron obovatum.

At 9,500 feet, Rhododendron arborea, majus, Abies cupressoides, Gaultheria nummularioides flexuosa, Thibaudiacea rotundifolia, Primula Stuartii, stunted juncus.

At 9,000 feet, Q. ilecifolia, Rhododendron undulatum, Primula pulcherrima, Tetranthera nuda, Chimaphiliæ! Andropogons, Rhododendron arbor, majus, common, which varies much in size of leaves, Dalibarda, Smilax ruscoideus.

At 8,500 feet, Berberis pinnata, asiatica, Buddlæa purpurea, Eurya acuminata.

At 8,000 feet, Gnaphalium trivenium, Baptisia, Spiræa, (Gillenioid) bella, Artemisia major. 7,500 feet, Rhododend. minus arborea, Leucas ciliata, and woods of Q. robur, as usual deciduous.

Sanah 7,983 feet.	—Q ilecifolia, Anhymenium, Rhodod. majus, Swertia, Juncus
Mica slate and gneiss.	—Primula Stuartii.
	—Abies, Brunonis, Rhodod. undulatum.
	—Baptisia, Primula Stuartii.
	—Abies cedroides, Thibaudia rotundifolia.
First ascent.	—Primula pulcherrima, Abies cedroides.
	—Daphne papyraceæ, Berberis, mosses abundant
	—Abies densa, Pedicularis, Spiræa.
	—Urticoidea, Betuloidea, Polygonum.
	—Rheum.
	—Abies densa, Rhododendron.
	—Betuloidea, Rhododendron.
Ridge composed of gneiss.	—Labiata, Xyris, Rosa.
Doonglala Peak 12,478 feet.	—Parnassia saxifraga, Pedicularis.
	—Abies densa.
	—Rosa.
	—Triticoides Polygonum,
	—Umbelliferæ.
	—Rhododendron pygmeum.
	—Xyris.
Sward	—Primula globosa, Umbellifera.
	—Dipsacus minor, Swertiæ.
	—Nardoides.
Halted for the night.	} Berberis ilecifolia, Tetranthera nuda, Rhodod. ferrugin. Betula, Abies.
Mica and talcose slate resting on gneiss.	—Brunonis cedroides, Rumex of Khegumpa.
	—Sphieropteris.
	—Chimaphila, Rhodod. majus, Q. ilecifolia.
Linge, 9,602 feet.	—Rhodod. minus, Artemisia major.

All the plants above 10,500 feet, had perished, not a single one being found in flower. The descent was so hurried, that it was impossible to note down more plants; and the same applies to the descent to this from the halting place. Starvation being to be added to discomfort.

Of Rhododendrons, the species observed, may be characterized as follows:—

Floribus in racemis umbelliformibus.

1. R. *arboreum*, arboreum, foliis oblongo obovatis, subtus argenteis.
2. R. *ferrugineum*, arboreum, foliis obovatis, supra rugosis, subtus ferrugineis.—No. 654.
3. R.————fruticosum, foliis oblongis, subtus ferruginea lepidotis.—No. 652.
4. R. *ellipticum*, fruticosum, foliis ellipticis.—No. 653.
5. R.————fruticosum, foliis ellipticis basi cordatis subtus glaucus reticulatis.—No. 659.
6. R.————fruticosum, foliis lanceolato oblongis, sub-obovatis, subtus punctatis.—No. 655.
7. R. *undulatum*, fruticosum, foliis elongati lanceolatis, undulatis subtus reticulatis.—No. 656.

Floribus solitariis.

8. R. *microphyllum*, fruticosum, lotum ferrugineo lepidotum, foliis lanceolatis parvis.

February 17*th*.—Snow has fallen during the night all around, but not within 1,000 feet of us: this will make the snow line here about 7,300 feet, the village being 6,335 *supra marem*. Mildness of climate would appear to be indicated by the abundance of rice cultivation round this place, chiefly, however, about 1,000 feet below. In every direction ranges of 9 to 12,000 feet are visible: villages are very common, especially so in a hollow on the western side of the ravine of the Kooree, in which I counted sixteen or eighteen; one containing between thirty and forty houses. The space alluded to is one sheet of cultivation, chiefly rice and wheat. Lingè itself is an ordinarily sized village, containing about twelve houses The wooded tracts cease for the most part, about 1,000 feet above this. The face of the country, where uncultivated, being clothed with harsh Andropogoneous grasses, Salix pendula, Thuja pendula, Pyrus malus, Erythrina, Quercus, Juncus effusus, Porana of Churra, Plantago, Barleria, Polygonium rheoides, Stellaria media, Rubus deltifoliis, Cnicus, Rhodod. arboreum minus, but rare, Smithea occurs also.

February 18th.—Our march commenced by a steep descent on the south face of the hill, the coolies proceeding by a more direct one to the north, but which was said to be difficult. We continued descending in a westerly direction, until we came in sight of the Kooree river which flows along the ravine, and which is a large stream, one-third less than the Monass. We then turned to the north following the river, the path running up, about 800 feet above it. We then came to another ravine, and descended to the torrent, which we crossed by a rude wooden bridge: then followed again the Kooree, to the bed of which we descended, and along which we continued for some time. We then ascended where the banks were of such a nature as not to allow a path, descending again here and there. Then we came on the Khoomun, a large torrent, which we crossed by a wooden bridge about 100 yards above its bed; re-descended to the Kooree, reached its bridge; and thence descending rather steeply, and for about one and a half mile to Ling-Ling, or Lengloon, which is plainly visible from the bridge over the Kooree.

After turning to the north along the Kooree, and indeed after passing the cultivation below Lingè, which chiefly occupies a sort of plateau, we passed through a most miserable country, the hills being rocky, nearly destitute of trees, and chiefly clothed with the usual coarse Andropogoneous grasses, especially lemon-grass, occurred between Lingè and Lengloon.

At 5,000 feet, observed Desmodium, Santalacea australasia, Gaultheria arborea, Indigofera, as before, Clematis cana, Acanthacea cærulescens, Pteris aquilina, Viburnum cærulescens, Oxyspora, Panicum eleusinoides, Anthestiria, Conyza, Ficus cordifoliis of Bhamree, Labiata Suddiensis, Corearia, Rhus pendula, Airoides major, Flemingia secunda and major

At 4,800 feet, Desmodium vestilum, stunted, Q. robur, Dipsacus, Epilobium, Elæagnus microphyllus, spinosus.

At 4,600 feet, Sedum, Campanula, Osbeckia capitata, Citrus in villages, Emblica, Artemisia minor.

At 4,000 feet, Pæderia cyanea, lemon-grass, Panax, Terebinthaceus, Pinus longifolia, here and there, Ficus obliqua, Grislea, Cirsium.

At the bed of the torrent 4,000 feet, Bassia.

Over the Kooree, Euphorbia antiqorum, a sure sign of aridity. Didymocarpea contorta, D. canescens, which differs from the other in being hirsute, Menispermum, Holcus elegans.

Along its bed, Sedum of Phoollong, Eugenia, Achyranthis, Ingoides arborea, Aspidium polypodioides, Briedleia obovata; Desmodium of Nulka! Arundo, Buddlæa neemdoides, Jasminum of Benka, Composita, involucri squamis ciliatis. Rice fields, in these Gnaphalium aureum, Phleoides of Tassangsee, but in full flower, Lysimachia majus, rugosus, Oxalis comiculata, Hieracioid, Composita, Lactucoid purpureseus, Ammannia, Bidens alba, Drymaria.

Then along the wooded banks, Wendlandia, *Pomacea?* Mimosa arborea, Camunium, Butea suffruticosa, Pterospermum of Bhamree, Luculia, Ulmus, as before, Pinus longifolia, Rottlera, Melica latifolia, young plants of Q. robur on rocks, along with it Goodyera articulata, Urticoid rhombifolia, carnosa; on rocks up Khoomun, Orthotrichum corcalypta. At the bridge over this, a Myrtaceous tree and the Simool occur. The plants occur during the ascent, as in the descent. Water-wagtails, blackbirds, tomtits, were observed, as also white-pated and white-rumped water-chats.

February 19th.—Ling-Ling or Lengloon.

February 20th.—To-day we visited the Soobah, who is a young man, certainly not more than twenty years old, with a good humoured countenance. The meeting was cordial but unattended with any state, and judging from appearances only, this Soobah is inferior to the others we have seen, and especially to him of Tassgong. No armed men were present, and the whole bystanders scarcely amounted to 100. It was agreed that we remain here until the baggage, now in the rear, arrives. Tonsa is, we hear, only four or five days journey from this.

The meeting took place in an open plot of ground below the Soobah's house and on the skirts of the village, the ground was matted and a space enclosed with mats: we sat in the open air; the Soobah under a silken canopy. Altogether he seemed a person of no pretensions, crowds, speaking comparatively, of priests attended as usual, they were the slickest looking of the whole, and the greatest beggars. A hideous party of *nachnees* were in attendance, and ready to perform any more pleasing duties they might be required; they were however so ugly, that not much self-denial was required in declining their offers. They were dressed in red, with abundance of cumbrous silver ornaments, and dirty leggings; one was additionally ornamented with incepient goitre.

Sugarcane (but stunted), almonds, or peach, oranges, castor-oil datura, pear, simool, may be found here. Oranges are poor enough, the pear no better. Pinus longifolia, Cùpressus pendula, are almost the only trees: the hills being barren, covered with coarse grasses.

February 23rd.—Marched to Tumashoo: our march commenced with a steep ascent, but which may be avoided by going through the village, it commenced and continued throughout in the direction of Lingè, opposite to which place we found ourselves on our arrival, but on the right bank of the river. The highest part reached, before we descended to this village, was 6,350 feet, or about the height of Lingè. The march was nearly six miles, it was easy, the road being throughout excellent and apparently more frequented than any we had hitherto seen. Generally we moved along through open Rhododendron woods, frequently very much stunted, at 6,000 feet. These were intermixed with Quercus tomentosa. The only spot well wooded, occurred in the ravines, giving exit to small streams.

The first ascent from Leng-Leng, gave the same vegetation, scarcely any trees being visible. Tradescantia clavijera of Churra on rocks, Galium of Churra, Santalacea, Desmodium vestilum, Indigofera canescens, Artemisia major and minor, Oxyspora, Luculia, Conaria, Sambucus in wet places, Lobelia pyramidalis, Spiræa bella and decomposita, Thalictrum majus, Gaultheria fruticosa, Woodwardia, Saurauja hispida, Rhododendron minus, and lemon-grass, occurred in the order of ascent.

Turning hence along the ridge at the same elevation, Gaultheria arborea, Quercus tomentosa, Rhododendron minus, Hedychium, Holcus elegans, Leucas ciliata. In wet wooded spots Gaultheria duplexa, Bucklandia, Viburnum cærulescens, Polyg. rheoides, Erythrina, Gordonia, Porana, Neuropeltis aromatica, Catharinea, Thibaudia myrtifolia, in open massy woods of Rhododendron minus and Quercus tomentosa, Rosa, Cnicus, Pyrus, Gleichenia major, Agrimonia occurred at the same elevations.

From one spot seven villages were visible, on opposite bank of Kooree and between Lingè and the Khoomun. A few stunted P. longifolia: one or two of Abies pendula, occurred 100 feet above the highest point of the former: at 6,350 feet, woods of the deciduous Q. robur, were observable.

On the descent at 6,000 feet, Mimosa spinosa, Primula Stuartii, Rhus, Juncus, and others, as before.

We passed several villages, some containing twenty or thirty houses, and on halting found ourselves towards the edge of the cultivated tract alluded to, as seen from Lingè.

Cattle are here kept in farm yards which are well littered with straw; as in other places they are noosed round the horns: they are fed, while tied up, on straw of a coarse and unnutritious description, which they do not seem to fancy much. Pigeons abound, but they are of no use as they cannot be caught; they may help to feed the sparrowhawks, which are generally found about the villages, and which are very bold.

February 24th.—Left at 8 A. M. after the usual trouble about coolies and ponies. We ascended at first about 1,000 feet, passing over sward with woods of P. longifolia on either side, crossing the ridge through a hollow, we then commenced a steep descent to the west, until we reached a water-course, the elevation of which is about 200 feet below that of Tumashoo. We then struck off, again to ascend, and continued to do so until we attained 7,800 feet, from which point we descended gradually at first, then abruptly to our *makan*. The direction was nearly west, the distance 11 miles, the march pretty easy, as the road was good, and the ascent gradual.

Up to the ravine and indeed throughout, nothing new occurred in the vegetation. The hill up which we ascended to again descend, was bare, covered with the usual coarse grasses, Campanula linearis and C. cana, foliis undulatis, Desmodium vestilum, Santalacea.

In the ravine Gordonia, Photinia, Pothos flammea and another species, Mæsa, Polygonum rheoides, Ficus of Bhamree, and in the *khets* Hieraceoid, Gnaphalium aureum, Ajuga, and Veronica occurred.

Up the first ascent and at about 5,500 feet, there was a field of peas, in very luxuriant condition. Our road lay through open dry woods of oaks, either Q. robur or Q. tomentosa, principally the latter, Rhododendron minus, and Pinus longifolia preponderated in some places, but few trees of Abies pendula occurred.

The march was so far interesting as establishing nearly the limits of Q. robur, Q. tomentosa and Q. ilecifolia, which last only commenced, and then in a small state, at 7,300 feet, I should say that Q. tomentosa was to it the next indication, as well as Q glauca. But it must be understood that only full grown trees are now considered. Mosses were common in the woods on reaching 6 to 7,000 feet, principally Dicrana, Hypna, Orthotricha, Pendulous lichens frequent; about 7,000 feet, Primula Stuartii in its old situations between 6 to 7,00 feet, Hypericum of Moflong, 7,000 feet.

We crossed several small water-courses, along these, the dry woods ceased, and the usual humid jungle made its appearance: mosses very numerous.

Lengloon 4,523 feet, mica slate.

.—Primula Stuartii.

Buddlæa purpurescens. .—Composita penduliflora.

At 7,300 feet, Quercus tomentosa, Ilecifolia glauca in wet places, Neckeræ. .—Shlotheimia, Chimaphilia, Daphne papyracum.

Scabiosa, Thibaudia myrtifolia. .—Didymocarpus canescens.

Bambusa microphylla. .—Gordonia, Berberis pinnata.

.—Smilax auriculata, Thalictrum majus.

Pinus longifolia. .—Spiræa decomposita, S. bella, Woodwardia.

Hills covered with Andropogoneous gramineæ: woods of Q. tomentosa, Q. robur, with Gaultheria arborea, fruticosa. .—Anthestiria.

Abies pendula, Viburnum *canum*, Pisum, Conarea. .—Indigofera canescens, Rubus delboideus.

.—Pothos, Q. Photinia, Gordonia.

In *khets* here Veronica, Hieraceoid Gnaphal. aureum, Ajuga. .—Mæsa.

Andropogons, Santalacea, Ficus cordifolia of Bhamree, Campanula linearis, canescens and undulata. .—Barren steep declivity.

.—Rhus pendula.

Traces of primary limestone. (Pemb.) .—Pinus longifolia.

Cultivation.

Tumashoo 5,000 feet, mica slate.

The above plants continued throughout, after reaching an altitude of 6,000 feet, the woods consisting of oaks and Rhododendrons.

The route for the most part wound along the course of the Kooree, but considerably above, we left this track about 3 P. M. on the river turning to the southward. Lingè was in sight nearly the whole day; we have been six days (including a halt) performing what might with ease be done in one, for there probably is a road in a direct line between this part and the opposite bank of Kooree. The small-crested finch, and red-beaked and red-legged fare occurred, the former is a noisy bird, inhabiting chiefly woods of Q. robur, the flock were loth to leave one particular spot, so that we obtained five specimens: the finch occurred at 7,800 feet.

Various temples and walls were passed en route, and a few villages, with one exception of average small size, were visible in various directions.

February 25th.—Our route hence continued for some time at about the same level, when we descended rather rapidly, until we reached a considerable stream, the Oongar, which is crossed by the ordinary wooden bridge; about 200 yards further, it is again crossed by means of a rude bridge, and the remainder of the march is a steep, long, and unmitigated ascent. I reached the tent about 5 P. M.; we passed one village situated near the larger bridge, with this exception the country seemed uninhabited: very little cultivation was visible in any direction.

The vegetation was the same, for the most part, the drier faces of the hills being covered, i. e. at about the level of Oongar, with oaks and Rhododendrons, the wet ravines being more densely, and more variously wooded. On sward about Oongar, I noticed a Pedicularis, Artemisia major, Stellaria angustifolia, Berberis pinnata in woods at the same elevation, Plantago, Crawfurdia speciosa, Rubus deltoideus, Alnus of Beesa, Otochilus, Gordonia, Lilium giganteum, Bucklandia.

In one spot near this place mosses were very abundant. On one rock I gathered, Weissiodes, Orthodon, Pohlia, Brachymenium bryoides, Weissia, Bartramioides, Didymodon, Daphne papyrifera, and Eurya acuminata, this being about the lowest elevation at which I have seen this plant. In cultivated spots Crucifera, Ervum, and at a temple about a mile from Oongar, Cupressus pendula, and a juniper, Arbor parva, of aspect scraggy, trunco lævi, Cannabis, Cerastium canum in cultivated places. The most common oak was Q. robur. The Jay, larger Brachypodium, which always goes in large flocks, orange-breasted Trochilus and blackbird, were likewise seen, as well as the brown finch, which was seen feeding on Rhododendron minus. On rocky ground I procured a really fine Acanthus, leaves all flesh-coloured, subscandens, spic. maximis lanato-ciliatis, tetrastich. on this the black cattle appear to be fed, as large bundles were brought in at Oongar. In the woody ravines Panax curcasifolia was common, in these I noticed Cerastium scandens, Elæagnus, Clematis, Tetrantheroidea habitu, Sedgewickiæ ! Orthotrichum pumulum ! Phlomoides, and in wet spots are Epilobium. The descent shewed nothing remarkable: towards the nullah I noticed Engelhaardtia, tree fern, and Gaultheria deflexa. Obtained a beautiful woodpecker at 5,000 feet, with the chesnut-pated lesser tomtit, Yunx, and speckled Brachypodium in woods here; this last has the habit and manners of the crooked bill of Dgin.

The wood between the two bridges was very pretty and open; the trees covered with mosses. The ascent shewed nothing remarkable until 2,000 feet had been surmounted, the plants forming the vegetation below this were Q. robur, Rhododendron minus in abundance, Thibaudia myrtifolia, Gaultheria arborea, Saurauja hispida uncommon, Viburnum cærulescens, Conyza nivea, Oxyspora towards the base with paper plant, and Bambusa microphylla. About 5,000 feet, a Daltonia, D. hypnoides, was found in abundance both on rocks and trees.

The change takes place about the situation of a spacious open sward; here the jungle is thick, the trees consisting principally of Q. glauca, which is a noble tree, with immense lamellated acorns. Pendulous lichens are here common, Hymenopogon parasiticus, Lomaria of Khegumpa ! Berberis asiatica ! Hemiphragma, Gaultheria nummulareoides, Panax Rhododendrifol.

At 7,500 feet, Rhododendron majus appears, the wood preserving the umbrageous humid aspect, Eurya acuminata, Hydrangea, and about this snow commenced sparingly, but soon became thick. At 8,000 feet, Rhododendron undulata, Tetrantheroides baccis nigris. At 9,000 feet, Rhododendron ferrugineum. The evening now became so misty that it was impossible to discern any thing; in addition, it was snowing: these circumstances added to fatigue made me press on for the halting place, before coming to which I passed through heavy snow.

Pémee, where we put up, is a miserable hut, is upwards of 9,000 feet above the sea, situated on an open sward, now densely covered with snow, the accommodations being of course very miserable. Icicles of large size were seen here; and we had nothing but snow for water.

February 26th.—Leaving this, we commenced a long and at last very steep ascent, the snow increasing in thickness as we increased our elevation, the march commenced with undulations, but soon passed off into an excessively steep ascent, in some parts indeed precipitous. We crossed at twelve and a half P. M. the Pass of Rodoola, on which are some slabs, with mystic characters, but even here the ascent did not terminate, but continued, although very gradually for perhaps two miles more. Before coming to the summit, a small hut is passed. The descent was at first very rapid, then we proceeded along the side of the mountain for a long way, at nearly the same level through woods of Abies densa. On recommencing the descent, swardy patches commenced, surrounded by fir woods, these increased in frequency. At length we reached extensive fir woods, from whence a valley was visible, percolated by a large stream to which we descended over open country with beautiful patches of firs, and at length over extensive swards. I reached the village at 5 P. M., after a march of nearly nine hours, the direction was west, the distance eighteen miles. The road was very bad; in one place our ponies escaped with difficulty, the road having apparently fallen in, and the only footing being afforded by the thickness of the snow: one poney was saved by placing branches under him. The highest portion of the Pass near the peak was good enough. Snow was heavy on the road, until we descended into the open fir-wooded country, it became scanty at 9,500 feet. The day was gloomy and misty, for a moment, the sun appeared while I stood on the summit, disclosing deep ravines, one formed by the valley in which we now are surrounded in every direction by equally high land, as that on which I stood, and certainly not under 12,000 feet. Nothing visible but dense forests of firs. The highest point crossed was 12,035 feet, estimating the summit to be 300 feet above the Pass itself, which is so narrow as scarcely to admit of the passage of a loaded mule.

In the open spot around the hut, Tofieldioid, which continues as high as 10,500 feet, Cerastium inflatum, Labiata species, Conecis, which, as on Dhonglaila, continues up to 12,000 feet, Dipsacus, Prunella, Gaultheria nummularioides, Pteris aquilina, stunted, Juncus niveus, Gnaphalium. No firs were visible, but the trees were so covered with snow, that I was not able to distinguish them.

At 9,800 feet, along an open ridge, Spiræa belloides, Buddlæa, B. purpurasæ, Khasyanæ affinis, Andropogones, Mespilus microphyllus, Hydrangea, Taxus, Swertia, Gnaphalium, Thibaudia orbicularis

2 I

commences, continuing up to 10,500 feet, Brachymenium bryoides, Bambusa very common, forming frequently the chief bulk of the forest, even up to 10,500 feet, Acer arbuscula foliis palmatum lobatis!! Pyrus arbor magna fol. obovat. serratis subtus albus, fructibus cerasi magnitudinum.

At 10,000 feet, Composita penduliflora! Hemiphragma, Lobelioides, Brachymenium bryoides, Rhododendron minus ferrugineum, arboreum vel arbuscula, Rhododendron obovatum, foliis subtus albus, Rhododendron hispidum, Rosa microphylla, Bambusa, Spiræa of former ascent.

At 10,200 feet, Polygonum, Rheum, Hydrangea! Spiræa belloides, Hydrangea, Betuloides.

At 10,500 feet, Abies densa, but sparingly, Rhododendron ellipticum, foliis basi cordatis, Hypericum, Rhododendron microphyllum.

At 11,000 feet, no firs: nothing almost but Rhododendrons, R. ellipticum, and R. ellipticum foliis basi cordatis.

At 11,500 feet, Vaccinium, foliis ovatis spinuloso-dentatis, atratus fructex pygmæus repens.

Towards the Pass, the face of the mountain became more and more rugged, the vegetation more scanty, consisting of nothing but Rhododendrons.

At 12,000 feet, Eriogonum minus, Polygonum, Rheum, Rhodod. microphyllum and ellipticum foliis basi cordatis.

About the Pass, Trichostomum, *Xyris*, Abies densa, one small plant, Rosa, Eriogonum minus, Rhododendron microphyllum and ellipticum foliis basi cordatis.

On the more level ridge between this Pass and the summit, Rhododendrons still were most frequent, Triticoides umbellifera of Royle, Eriogonum majus, woods of Abies densa occurred a little below the path, Gentiana maxima, 4-pedalis folliculis bipollicaribus, Lilium uniflorum, Potentilla common between this and 9,000 feet, Rosa microphyllum, Juniperus, Epilobium minus of Dhonglaila, Rheum. Large black crow, Pedicularis, Saxifraga, Umbellifera alia, Compositæ, Spiræa.

At the summit, no woody vegetation was visible, except Rhododendrons; the firs being confined below.

The descent at first through Rhododendron, then for a long time entirely through vast woods of Abies densa, most of the larger trees of this are apparently blasted, it has a tabular form, and very sombre appearance, and can be recognized even at great distances by its black columnar palm-like appearance.

At 11,000 feet, Acer sterculiacea, Rosa microphylla, Ribes, which ceases below 10,000 feet, it is confined to the A. densa woods.

At 10,500 feet, Saxifraga, two species on moist banks, A. densa woods, small Umbellifera.

The sward commences at about 10,000 feet, and is common at 9,500 feet. It is clothed principally with the small bamboo noticed in similar places above Sanah. Berberis spathulata commences. It is with this sward that a new fir, with a larch-like look, which I call temporarily Abies spinulosa, commences, and continues down to the nullah, becoming more abundant as A. densa becomes less abundant, and finally usurping its place entirely. Rhododendron microphyllum continues to 9,600 feet, at which point Baptisoidea commences.

The vegetation hence to Bhoomlungtung consists entirely of Abies spinulosa, intermixed with a species very like Abies pendula, this appears at about 9,500 feet. The sward consists of small grasses, Juncus niveus, Gnaphalium, Hypericum of Moflong, suffrutex incertus, Juncus effusus at 9,000 feet, with Prinsepia utilis.

The marked indicators of great elevation are A. densa, Polygonum, Rheum! Eriogona! Rhododendron microphyllum, ellipticum, and ellipticum foliis basi cordatis, Epilobium, Triticoides, Holcoides, Umbellifera of Royle, Saxifragæ, Ribes, Juniperus.

The most marked peculiarity is the comparative absence of A. densa on the east side of the mountain, and its excessive abundance on the west. This valley may be justly called the valley of pines, for in no direction is any forest to be seen but those composed of pines. The change indeed is extraordinary, in other respects as indicated by the presence of a new Rosa and Prinsepia utilis. Another peculiarity is the appearance for the first time of A. spinulosa. The range of which is between 8 to 10,000 feet; this is a beautiful tree, and disposed in beautiful groups. The valley altogether is a beautiful one, and actually repays one for the trouble endured in getting access to it.

The temperature in crossing the ridge was below that on Dhonglaila, and below the freezing point at times. No inconvenience was felt by us from the elevation, but many of our servants suffered probably as much from fright as cold.

February 27th.—Halted.

February 28th.—This valley is certainly the prettiest place we have yet seen, the left bank is particularly level, but neither are of much breadth, the hills adjacent present rounded grassy patches, interspersed with beautiful groves of pines. The level space, as well as the more favourable sites on the slopes of the hills, are occupied by wheat cultivation, which is carried on in a more workman-like manner, than any of the previous cultivation I have hitherto seen. The fields are occasionally surrounded with stone walls, but generally only protected from the inroads of cattle by branches of thorny shrubs strewed on their edges. They are kept clean, and above all, manure is used: it is however dry and of a poor quality, apparently formed of animal and vegetable moulds. In some of the fields the surface is kept very fine, all stones and clods being carefully removed and piled up in various parts of the field, but whether these masses are again strewed over the ground. The plough is used, and penetrates to about four inches. Hoes and rakes are also used, but the angle of the handle is much too acute. Radishes are grown with the wheat: no rice is cultivated here.

The village Bhoomlungtung, at which we are stationed is, on the left bank of a branch of the Bhoomla nullah, a river of some size, but fordable in most places, its bed being subdivided. It is 8,668 feet above the sea. The houses are ordinary, but they are surrounded with stone walls. Our's, which is a portion of the Dhumpas or headman's, has a court-yard, surrounded by a stone wall, and the entrance is defended by a stout and large door. The natives invariably wear dark clothing, the colour being only rivalled by that of their skins, for I never saw dirtier people. The Bhooteas hitherto visited, were quite paragons of cleanliness compared to those we are now among. Half ruined villages are visible here and there, although otherwise the appearance of the valley is prosperous enough. The valley is surrounded on all sides by hills of great altitude, the lowest being 10,500 feet high. Snow is plentiful on the ridges, but it does not remain long below, although falls are frequent. No fish are to be seen in the river, which is otherwise as regards appearance as beautiful a trout stream as one could wish to have. The birds are the common sparrow, fieldfare, red-legged crow, magpie, skylark, a finch which flies about in large flocks, with a sub-forked tail, raven, red-tailed stonechat, larger tomtit, syras, long-tailed duck, and quail, which is much larger than that found in Assam. The woods are composed entirely of Abies pendula, a few A. spinulosa occur, intermixed, but the woods of the latter species are scarcely found below 9,500 feet. The ridges are clothed with the columnar Abies densa. In thickets a smaller Rosa, Rhododendron ellipticum, foliis basi cordatis, Rhododendron elliptica, foliis subtus argenteis, Rhodod. gemmis viscosis. Berberis asiatica, Hamamelidea? Bambusa microphyllum, Philadelphus, Thibaudia orbicularis, Mespilus microphyllus, Taxus or Abies Brunonis, Ilex dipyrena, occur. The sward shews small grasses, all past flower, Hemiphragma, Thymus, Dipsacus, Juncus niveus, Gnaphalia 2, 3, Potentilla.

The fields have Crucifera Lamium and Verbascum, a late biennial species, Caule simplici, Hemiphragma.

The marshy spots abound with Juncus effusus, and shew also a Primula out of flower, and a Xyris past flowering.

Along the bed of the river, Hippophae is the most common plant. Lastly, a few trees occur of Q. ilecifolia, which assumes a very handsome character, looking much like a Conifera at some distance, one group occurs near the village, and a solitary tree or two elsewhere. The other woody vegetables are Rosa fructibus hispidis, Cycnium, Pomacea arbuscula, and one or two other deciduous shrubs. The willow tree is also common.

March 1*st*.—Marched to Byagur, we were told that the march was a short one, and that we should continue throughout along the Bhoomlungtung river, which is called Tung-chiew. We did keep along this for about two miles, when we struck off into the hills: passing through a village, we continued rising for perhaps 1,000 feet, when we descended to a small nullah. Leaving this we commenced an ascent, and a very long one too, and continued to ascend until we surmounted the ridge overlooking the river, on which Byagur or Iugur is situated. To the place we descended, the march was fourteen miles, direction westerly. Highest ground traversed about 9,500 feet high. Road throughout winding round and up hills, through woods of Abies pendula: nothing of interest occurred. Magpies, crows, chatterer feeding on pine cones, common in woods at 9,000 feet. Passed two or three villages, all containing ruined houses. Direction we pursued was that of the Tung-chiew river, until we reached the ridge guiding the Byagur river to it: their junction takes place two or three miles below this place, Cycnium occurred on the road in plenty, also Sarcococea.

Horseshoe curlew, the same as we shot at Daimara, common in the Tung-chiew, along which the chief shrubs are Hippophae and Elæagnus, particularly in the islets which are not uncommon in its bed. The common water wagtail also occurs.

I find that the root of the common Potentilla is used here, as about Nunklow, as a substitute for *sooparee*, it is unpleasantly astringent.

Observed Rhododendron microphylla on the loftier ground; very high land, 18,000 feet visible to the south along the course of Tung-chiew, covered with heavy snow: Abies pendula is occasionally a beautiful tree, 100 feet high, and in appearance something like a cedar, the finest occurs at a monastery under a bluff rock, about one and a half mile from Bhoomlungtung on the Tung-chiew; Daphne papyriferæ occurred at 9,000 feet. The heaps of earth piled up in the fields before sowing, consist of burnt rubbish, the ashes are subsequently spread out. The manure consists entirely of vegetables: here I find that the pine leaves are piled up, and formed into manure by fermentation.

March 2nd.—Byagur, the Soobah's house is about 500 feet above us, and is a huge rambling edifice. We are in a village situated in a rather capacious valley, percolated by a large river, twice the size of the Tung-chiew, which is crossed by an ordinary bridge, the river runs close to the hills, which form the left bank, the right is a sort of plain, occupied by wheat cultivation, and which has apparently at a former period, been the bed of the river. In this valley other villages are visible, but they are small, and nothing indicates either fertility or prosperity. The valley is surrounded on all sides by high mountains, those towards Bhoomlungtung being lowest. To the north-east very high land is visible. The ridge which separates us from Tongse is, in the highest parts, certainly 12,000 feet, and covered with snow. The people are dirty to an excess.

Crow, sparrow, Alauda, are the birds here. Saw a fox, an animal of some size, with a beautiful brush. The botany is poor, the hills are clothed with the usual grasses, abundance of Abies pendula. The khets or fields present the old Lamium and Crucifera. The only trees are one of Q. ilecifolia, and one or two of Salix lanata.

March 3rd —Cycnium is found here, but is put to no use. The crops which are now springing up are very poor, the soil being extremely bad, they are irrigated by means of canals, but terraces are not in use, the ground being too level, the embankments are much smaller than those used in rice cultivation.

The place is bleak in the extreme, and here, as often on the western face of the Himalaya, at this season a fierce diurnal wind rises directly the sun gets power, which always blows up the ravines or against the streams; draining these, it dies away towards evening, generally. It is cold in the extreme, and must check vegetation extremely. Syras, common here, as at Bhoomlungtung.

The ridge above this which is crossed coming from Bhoomlung-tung, is 9,947 feet high, yet no snow was on the ground. The contrast between it and Pèmee in regard to snow and vegetation is remarkable; there the woods were thick, luxuriant, and varied, here nothing is to be seen but Abies pendula. I consider this a proof that A. pendula is a native of places below much snow, and that where snow abounds, it will not be found to extend above 8,000 feet. The dwarf bamboo of Sanah is common here, covering large patches of ground, Lamium of Bulphai in the vicinity of temples, and enclosing pagodas. The people here evince great skill in figures, but none in architecture.

The Soobah's house a castillated heterogeneous mansion, spread over much ground, the defences on one side reaching nearly to the level of the valley. The Kumpa dogs are fierce and handsome, with the bark of a mastiff, they are not apparently deterred by threats, but rather the contrary. A woman with dropsy, wrapped in filthy clothes, presented herself and evinced great anxiety to have her pulse felt, but the dirt of her clothes was such, that I made excuses.

Manure for the land consists of pine leaves, etc. mixed with cow-dung. The cattle are well littered; and grass is here of rather better description: all cattle are however in wretched condition notwithstanding, and the cows give very little milk. The houses of the poorer orders, are unornamented, but those of the better classes are always ornamented with a belt of red ochre outside. There are no large boulders in the river here, although it runs with violence. This is owing to the softness or tenacity of the rocks.

March 4th.—Our march commenced with a steep ascent up the ridge, forming the west boundary of the valley, surmounting this we proceeded on for some distance at about the same level, and thence descended rapidly to a nullah. We then ascended slightly, and subsequently descended to the valley, in which the village Jaisa is situated. The distance was nine miles; the march was pretty, almost entirely through fir woods, three villages were visible in a valley to the left, which is in fact the termination of the Jaisa one, but beyond the valleys no cultivation whatever was visible.

The first part was up a barren grassy slope, after which we entered fir woods, these at first were almost entirely constituted of Abies pendula.

At 9,000 feet Chimaphila, Berberis spathulata, Abies pendula, Bambusa microphylla of Sanah, Mespilus microphyllus, Rhododendron elliptica, foliis basi cordatis subtus argenteis, Philadelphus Lycopod. of Surureem, Gaultheria nummularifolia, Rhododendron viscosum.

At 9,300 feet, Abies spinulosa becomes more common, Rosa hispida and microphylla! Pinus cedroides commences, Dalibarda, Daphne papyracea, Thymus, Gnaphalia, Mespilus and Berberis, as before, Potentilla.

At 9,500 feet, snow lying on the path in sheltered places, Euphorbia, Gaultheria arboreoides, Hypnum rubescens, scolopendrioids, Pteris aquilina, Melianthus, Rosa, frutex erectus ramis hispidissimis, ramulis subglabratis, fructibus pendulis glabris, tubo-ovato, sepalis lanceolatis. Salix arbuscula, gemmis rubur glabris, foliis lanceolatis subtus glaucis, amentis fæminies pendulis, Bupleurum, Hydrangea, Spiræa densa belloides! Prunella, Pinus cedroides common at Potentilla.

At 9,700, 9,800, to 10,000 feet, Abies densa, a few trees, as usual many blasted, from lightning confined entirely towards the summit, Acer stercuilacea, Aruncus, Thibaudia orbicularis, A. spinulosa very common, A. pendula ceases, or at most only stunted plants occur, Mespilus microphyllus, Berberis spathulata, Baptisia, these were very common on west face, which is level enough and open.

Here also Pedicularis, Bupleurum, stunted Pteris aquilina, Polygonum, Rheum! Avena! Pendulous lichens luxuriant. Along the level tracts, the woods consisted entirely of Abies spinulosa, a minute Gentiana common on the sward.

The descent was steep to the ravine; half-way down A. pendula commenced to flourish, and towards the ravine it was more common than A. spinulosa, Rhododendron microphyllum was seen on this face at 9,500 feet, Verbascum at 9,200 feet, but most of the plants seen on the east face were not found on this. Acer sterculiacea, however occurred at 9,800 feet, otherwise pines were the most prominent feature.

At the nullah, Dipsacus, Elæagnus, Salix lanata, Artemisia major, Daphne papyracea, Rhododendron viscosum, Mespilus microphyllus, Rosa hispida, spinus acutissimis, Bambusa of Sanah, Plectranthus a large suffruticose annual species, common in all the same altitudes, were observed. The subsequent descent was through woods of A. pendula, with a few of A. spinulosa intermixed.

The limits of A. densa, A. spinulosa and A. pendula, Melianthus, Acer sterculiacea, Thibaudia orbicularis, A. cedroides, Rosa microphylla, Pedicularis, Hydrangea, Baptisia, Berberis spathulata were well determined. They may be expressed as follows : A. densa, 10 to 13,000 feet, A. spinulosa, 9 to 10,500 feet, A. pendula, 6 to 9,000 feet, Melanthus, 9,500 feet, Acer sterculiaceum, 9,800 to 10,000 feet, Thibaudia orbicularis, 10,000 feet, A. cedroides, 9,000 to 9,800 feet, Rosa microphylla, 9,800 to 13,000 feet, Pedicularis, 10 to 12,500 feet, Hydrangea, 4 to 10,000 feet unless two species are confounded, Baptisia, 9 to 9,800 feet, Berberis spathulata, 9 to 10,000 feet.

Jaisa is a good sized village for Bootan, and the houses are rather large. We were lodged in the castle, a large building, with a capacious flagged court-yard, surrounded by galleries : we were housed in the grand floor of the higher portion fronting the gate. A good deal of wheat cultivation occurs around. The village is situated in a small nullah, surrounded on all sides by pine-clad hills. The vegetation is precisely the same as at Juggur, with the exception of a Ligustrum, which is common along the nullah. Larks, red-legged crows and ravens, abound here.

March 5th.—Our march consisted of a progress along levelish ground up the river, occasionally rounding small eminences : we then commenced the ascent of a ridge, the summit of which we reached about half past-twelve. Snow is common above 9,000 feet. The descent was steep and uninterrupted from about 2,000 feet, when we reached a small river. Thence we ascended a little to descend again, we continued over a ravine at nearly the same level, for sometime proceeding over undulated ground : on reaching the debouchure of the ravine into a larger one running north and south, we commenced to descend rapidly until we came to an elevation situated above Tongsa, to this place the descent was excessively steep. The march was thirteen miles long, the direction west.

At a temple near Jaisa found the Juniper of Oongar in flower, and arboreous, attaining a height of about 40 feet. The whole march up, nearly to the summit, was through pine woods, A. pendula and spinulosa being intermixed for sometime. I noticed Primula globifera, Eucalypta, Thibaudia orbicularis, Aruncus, Rosa ramis hispidis, Dipsacus, Prunella, Potentilla, Gnaphalium, Sphagnum, Daphne papyracea, Tofieldia, Gaultheria nummularoides, as we approached the base of the ridge or rather the spot at which the ascent commenced. At this place Abies cedroides commenced, and Abies pendula became uncommon.

On a bank here, I gathered abundance of mosses Bartramia, Dicrana, etc. and some Jungermanniæ.

The ascent was through precisely similar vegetation, in one place it was exceedingly pretty, consisting of sward with pines. Here snow was lying on the ground in sheltered places to the depth of several inches. The ground hence was levelish, but between this place and the summit a rise of a hundred feet took place. Between these places Abies densa, cedroides and spinulosa, occurred, but this was uncommon, Rosa ramis hispidis, Salix of yesterday, Bambusa of Sanah, stunted Pteris aquilina, Betuloidea, Hydrangea, Hypnum rufescens, scolopendrioid as well as below: Spiræa belloides, Rhododendron obovatum, which varies on the same plant with ferruginous and white leaves, Sphagnum, Thibaudia orbicularis. On sward Gentiana minima.

As the snow increased, Abies cedroides became less, Abies densa more common. At the very summit Parnassia, Polygonum rheum, Composita penduliflora, Rhododendron hispidum, Berberis spathulata, which had occurred previously, Vaccinium pumilium, ciliatum, Gentiana minima, Swertia, Cnicus, Compositæ frequent, Labiata spicata of Dhonglaila.

The descent was at first open, through swardy places: here Acer sterculiaceum, Geranium scandens, Avena, Abies densa, Juniperus fruticosa, raro arbuscula.

At 9,800 feet, Rhododendron foliis lanceolato-oblongis subtus ferruginea tomentosis, arborea, became very common, forming large woods, Abies densa interspersed, Juniperus, Betuloidea which has six or seven layers of bark, the *boj-putah* of Hindoostan according to Blake, Rosa microphylla, Hemiphragma, Daphne papyracea, Dicranum atratum, etc.

At 9,500 feet, Clematis, Berberis asiatica, commences, Betula, common Andropogoneous grasses.

At 9,300 feet, Primula pulcherrima, Abies cedroides very common, Abies densa ceasing, Buddlæa purpurescens, Aruncus, Bupleurum.

At 9,200 feet, Lonicera villosa, Vaccinium cyaneum, Bambusa alia, Abies densa ceasing.

At 9,000 feet, the jungle now became humid, Gaultheria flexuosa, Mespilus microphyllus, Quercus ilecifolia, Tetrantheroides baccis nigris, Gaultherium nummularifolia common, Rubia cordifolia! Hydrangea.

At 8,900 feet, Junipers ceases, woods of Q. ilecifolia and Pinus cedroides, Rosa microphylla, shrubby Rhododendrons, that which was arboreous previously now becoming shrubby, Berberis asiatica,

Taxus or Abies brunonis! Lomaria of Khegumpa, Rhododendron foliis oblongis subtus punctatis ferrugineis, Rubus, Primula Stuartii! Quercus folliis, Castaneæ, Ilex, Betuloid, continues.

At 8,500 feet, Panax rhododendrifolia, Thibaudia obovata, Taxus ophiopogon angustissimus, Rhododendron formosum majus! Smilax ruscoideus vel gaultherifolia! Primula pulcherrima, very common.

At 8,200 feet, Spiræa decomposita, Thibaudia obovata very common. No firs, woods of oaks and Rhododendron majus, Panax rhododendrifolia and another species; Bambusa.

At the nullah, same vegetation, Tetranthera nuda, Primula pulcherrima, Valeriana violifola, Eurya acuminata, Daphne papyrifolia, Fragaria, Potentilla supina, Rumex of Khegumpa, Poa annua, Stellaria media and angustifolia, Rhodoracea deflexa!

At 8,000 feet, the woods at this elevation have the same characters, Rhododendron argenteum becomes common, Q. ilecifolia and Castaneæ facies, both very handsome and large trees, covered with pendulous mosses, Sphæropteris, Saxifragea viridis, fleshy Urticea, Oxalis major on sward at the same elevation, Vaccinium cyaneum, Mespilus microphyllus, Artemisia major, Gnaphalium, Dipsacus, Elæagnus in woods, Tetranthera nuda, Taxus, Gaultheria flexuosa nummularifolia, Vaccinium cyaneum, Lomaria, Lonicera villosa, paper plant, Thibaudia orbicularis, Hedera.

At 7,800 feet, towards open barren hills, Indigofera canescens, Q. robur, Spiræa decomposita, Anthistiria minor, Composita penduliflora, Alnus of Beesa, Juncus effusus, Viburnum cærulescens, Xyris, Scripus fuscescens of Tassangsee, Gaultheria arborea and fruticosa, Polygonum rheoides, Smilax auriculata, Saccharum aristata, Lobelia pyramidalis, Stauntonia latifolia, Salix lanata, Deutzia.

At 7,500 feet, Quercus tomentosa commences, between this and Tongsa, Berberis asiatica is very common, Rosa sp., quarta, Cyaneum dycopod. of Surureem, Ilex dipyrena, Tuipus, Kysoor of Churra, Apple, Gleichenia major, Rubus deltoideus. In wheat fields, 7,500 feet, Crucifera, Thlaspa, Lamium, Ervum, are found, Vaccinium cyaneum continues to 7,000 feet, this Mespilus microphylla, Berberis asiatica, Cycnium, Lycopod. of Surureem, Ilex, Daphne papyriferæ, are the only elevational plants found between 8 and 9,000 feet, and which continue low down. All the others ceased with the jungles.

March 13th.—Tongsa: this, although the second place in the kingdom, is a poor wretched village, the houses, always excepting the palace, are poorer than ordinary, abounding in rats, fleas, and other detestable vermin. Our reception would seem to be uncordial: we are miserably housed in the heart of the village, which is a beggarly one. On descending the hill some people in the Pillo's house behaved very insolently, roaring out, and making most insolent signs for me to dismount, of which of course I took no notice: sparrow-hawk was seen at 8,000 feet. There is but little cultivation, indeed the adjoining hills are barren in the extreme. The little cultivation there is of barley, which is now in the ear, and decent enough; the crops being much better than any we have yet seen, although in many fields it is difficult to see any crop at all. The village, including the houses on the surrounding adjoining heights does not contain thirty houses. There is one flock of sheep, which are in good condition, some small shawl-goats, and a few cattle, but of a lighter breed than the Mithans, from which they are very distinct, and which we have scarcely seen since crossing Dhonglaila, the first high ridge. There is some rice cultivation along the nullah or torrent, on which the village is situated. Pears, peaches likewise occur, and are now both in flower. The hills around are bare, nothing but shrubby vegetation being visible, the tree-jungle not descending below 7,500 feet, except on one spur to the south-west, on which it reaches nearly to our present level.

The shrubby vegetation consists of Hamamelidæ, Salix, Gaultheria fruticosa, Rosa, Rubus, Pomacea, Elæagnus, Berberis asiatica, among which Artemisia major occurs on sward. Primula Stuartii, Potentilla and P. supina, Oxalis acetoseltoides, Juncus, Bartramia, Polytrichum glaucum, Fragaria vesca. In the fields Lamium, Crucifera, Thlaspi, Gnaphalium aureum, Prenanthoid, Fragaria indica, Viola, Ranunculus, Oxalis acetosella, Poa annua.

Urtica urens, and urentior occur about the houses, Cupressus pendula and a Magnoliaceous tree, with exquisitely fragrant blossoms.

The palace is a huge, long, straggling piece of patch-work, of ordinary construction, and less imposing than that of Byagur, which the Pillo makes his summer residence on the Bhoomlungtung; it is however ornamented with three gilt umbrellas. It is situated on the bank of the nullah, and defended by some outworks, 6 to 700 feet above it; to the east, these might, from their situation, be easily demolished by stones. The palace itself is commanded in every direction, particularly by the hill, along which we came from Jaisa; indeed a person might jump from the summit of this on to the outpost, and thence on to the palace; so precipitous is the descent.

The people, above all those hitherto seen, are dirty in their persons, uniting curiosity with no small share of obstinacy and impertinence in their manners. The birds are the blackbird, a black mina, the house-sparrow, sparrow-hawk, larger crow, domestic pigeons, kites, and hoopoo. The red-legged crows I have heard once, but far above, nor do I think that they ever visit this. The productions being essentially different from those of the elevated valleys we have lately quitted. Can those valleys be the *steps* to the table-land of Thibet to which they must be near, and which is reached sooner in that direction than any other? The idea of the high vallies in question being steps to table-land is perhaps corroborated by the fact, that the table-land is said to be within two days' journey from Byagur.

Our interview with the Pillo took place on the 15th, it was conducted with some state, and with some impertinence. The latter was indicated by delaying us at the door of the audience room, the former by the attendance of more numerous and better dressed attendants than usual. Two Pillos were present. The incense as usual was burning, and the Pillos, both old and new, were seated before some large Chinese-looking figures. The only novel ceremony was the praying over a mess of something which I imagine was meant for tea; in the prayer all joined, when finished the beverage was handed to the Pillos, who, however, were contented with merely tasting it. Before this some was strewn on the floor in front, and some to the right of the chieftains. The castle was in places crowded with people, no less than 5 to 600, but all were as dirty as usual. None but the immediate attendants appeared armed. The new Pillo is a dark low-looking man, with an incipient goitre, the old one a more decent aristocratic looking person, good-looking and very fair. The presents were of course beggarly, consisting of indifferent oranges, wretched plantains, sugarcane of still worse quality, and ghee of an abominable odour.

March 17*th.*—We still remain here, and do not expect to leave for two or three days. The weather is unsettled, and the sun increasing in power daily. The new Soobahs left to-day for their appointments, with the exception of the Dewangur one. Pigs are here fed on boiled nettle leaves: old ladies may be seen occasionally busily employed in picking the leaves for this purpose, and which they do by means of bamboo pincers or tweezers. A few plantains may be met with here, but in a wretched state. Rice may be seen 500 feet above this, on the north of the castle, the slope of a hill being appropriated to its cultivation; the terraces above, owing to the inclination, are very narrow, and from the paucity of straw, the crops must, I should infer, be very poor.

March 22*nd.*—To-day we took our leave of the Pillo, who received us in a room to the south of the castle. He was friendly enough, but begged for presents unconscionably. He was surrounded by a considerable number of more mean looking persons than ordinary. On the previous meeting he talked openly of being at enmity with the present Deb Rajah, but on this occasion he said little on the subject.

The castle is an ill-built, and worse arranged building, the windows and loopholes being so placed as to afford every facility for shooting into the air. In a court-yard, several tiger skins brought from the plains, are suspended.

It now appears that this Pillo, who said previously that the new Deb was never installed, is himself an usurper, previously handing the old Deb from the throne. This latter personage appears to be by far the more popular of the two. The Pillo must now have great influence, as all the posts in his division, are either held by his own sons, or by his more influential servants. The sons by the bye are, so long as they remain in the presence, treated like ordinary servants. Joongar is held by one of his sons, a lad of about eighteen, of plain but pleasing appearance and of good manners. He visited us yesterday, and his newly acquired rank sat easily on him. The old Pillo no doubt owes his rank to his having been the father of the lad chosen to be Dhurma Rajah, he is himself very evidently low-born and low-bred, and compared with the former one, so poor a specimen, that the greater popularity of the former is not to be wondered at. From all we have heard, they are contemptible rulers, as they appear to do nothing but intrigue for power among themselves. Changes are hence excessively frequent, and were they attended with much bloodshed, the country would be depopulated.

This evening we had ample proof that the Bhootea houses are not water-proof. Heavy showers occurred with thunder and dense clouds from the south-west.

March 23*rd.*—We left Tongsa, proceeding through the castle, and thence struck down to the river Mateesun. The descent was very steep, and amounted to about 1,200 feet. The river is crossed by an ordinary bridge, it is a large and violent stream and contains fish, some of which, seen by Blake, were of large size. Crossing this, we continued throughout the remainder of the march, gradually rising along the ridges bounding the Tongsa river. We continued rising until we reached our halting place, Taseeling. In one or two places, the road was completely built up; ascending by zig-zags up, in some degree, perpendicular cliffs. The distance was seven miles.

Proceeding to the bridge, observed Rubus deltoideus, Pomacea, Quercus tomentosa, Artemisia major, Cycnium, Gaultheria arborea and fruticosa, Buddlæa, Quercus altera, Indigofera cana, Gaylussacia serratoides, Hedera, Thibaudia myrtifolia, Pomacea sauraugifolia, Viburnum cærulescens, Quercus robur budding, Pterogonium, Fragaria, Duchesnia.

The remaining hills were much similar, generally very bare, clothed with partial woods of Q. tomentosa, Rhododendron minus; the oak changing to Q. robur, as we increased our elevation. Near the bridge noticed Bucklandia, Erythrina, which is likewise found at Tongsa, Maesa salicifolia, Urena lobata, Cnicus, Mimosea! Arbuscula inermis, Senecio scandens in flower, Araliacea subscandens, Didymocarp. contort., a Solenia, Betuloideus, Panax curcifolia, Alnus, Arundo, Anthistiria arundinacea, Cerasus, Tricerta unisexualis, at 6,000 feet.

At about the same elevation Rhododendron minus becomes common, Primula Stuartii, Dipsacus, Verbenacea exostemma, Scleria, Valeriana, Tradescantia on rocks, with Saxifraga ligularia in full flower at 6,500 feet.

About this, 6,500 to 6,800 feet, Spiræa decomposita, Hamamelidea here a tree, occasionally but small, Erythroxyloides, Conyza nivea and communis, Gleichenia major, Parochetus communis on wet dripping rocks, Woodwardia, Clematis ternata.

At 7,000 feet, Berberis asiatica, Q. tomentosa ceased, its place being supplied by Q. robur, Verbascum, Juncus, Gaultheria nummularioid, Mespilus microphyllus, Scirpus fuscus of Tassangsee, Thibaudia gaultherifolia, Rubia cordifolia, Azalea, and Daphne capitulis pendulis, Ranunculus uniflorus, Hydroctyle.

Taseeling is situated about 2,000 feet above the Mateesun, on a nakedish hill; about it there is some cultivation, and one or two villages, one towards Tongsa and above Taseeling of some size. The place itself consists of a large house, with some fine specimens of Cypressus pendula, the east face of the house has the red stripe, indicative of rank. Its elevation is about 7,300 feet, close to the house I observed the Lamium of Bulphai, Bursa pastoris, Oxalis corniculata, Cnicus out of flower, Artemisia major, Fragaria vesca, Daphne pendula and papyracea, Hemiphragma, Composita pendulifolia, Lycopod. of Surureem, Hypericum, Berberis asiatica, Juniperus; Barley cultivation, and a Pomaceous arbuscula, armat. ovar. 5-discretis. The red-legged crow occurs here, and a thrush much resembling our English one. The raven of course occurs. A curious opening occurs in the hills at Taseeling, affording a prospect of the Bag Dooar plains, seven days' journey distant, but the road is bad.

March 24th.—Leaving Taseeling we commenced to ascend until we rounded a ridge, when we turned to the west, we then commenced to descend, but slightly, winding over undulated surfaces of barrenish hills. After sometime we reached heavy tree jungle, the road proceeding in the same undulating manner, so that it was impossible to say whether we had risen or descended. About one we came on the river, up the ravine of which we had been advancing ever since turning to the west. This stream is of some size, very violent and rapid, but fordable. Near this is a large pagoda, built after the old Boodhistical style, and the only respectable one we have yet seen, its site is pretty, and it is ornamented above with eyes and a fiery-red nose. Leaving this we ascended along one bank of the river, until we reached Chindupjee, our halting place; this was distant from the pagoda three miles, and from Taseeling twelve. This latter part reminded me of Bhoomlungtung; firs being the prevailing trees, and the valley having more pretensions to the name than usually happens.

We encamped in a beautiful spot, the house being situated on fine sloping sward, surrounded by picturesque trees of Q. ilecifolia, a few tall Cypressus standing up in the centre. The village is a few feet above, and of average size, although it looks from a little distance to be of considerable size. The march throughout was beautiful, especially after entering the wooded tract; this reminded me of the march near Khegumpa, the woods were here and there very picturesque, glades and swards abounding, water was very abundant here, and this no doubt causes the development of so much vegetation.

At 7,800 feet, Thibaudiaceæ very common, Rhododendron two species, Gaultheria flexuosoides, Thibaudia obovata, Caudata myrtifolia, Hydrangea, which I find to be a climber, Rhododendron majus, commencing, pine wood; chatterers heard here. Hills naked or covered here and there with stunted wood; marshy places common.

From a sketch made on the spot by W. Griffith. M & N Hanhart, lith Printers.

At 7,600 feet, Lomaria of Khegumpa, Tetranthera nuda, Sphæropteris, pear and apple, Q. tomentosa, Magnolia grandiflora begins, Polygonum rheoides, Daphne pendula, which is used, as well as the other, both here and in Nipal in the manufacture of paper: brick-red black-pate.

At this same elevation farther on, Rosa hispida! Gillenia, Juncus, Rhododendron deflexa, Smilax gaultherifolia, Spiræa bella, Dipsacus, Spiræa decomposita, Ilex, Vaccinium cyaneum, Magnolia grandiflora very common. The country now becomes more wooded, the woods being confined to moist ravines, and in other situations where water is very plentiful, the woods throughout become continuous, and forming the large forests before mentioned: having the open spaces between the woods covered with sward, on which Gentiana pygmæa, and Fragaria are very common.

As we approached the wood or forest, Pinus cedroides commenced, and towards the valley of Chindupjee this species became very common, Rumex occurred throughout in wet places, also at Taseeling. Geranium is common also in wet places, Stauntonia latifolia, Potentilla, Duchesnoides, Tussilago of Churra, on the confines of wood and on it. Here the orange-breasted trochilus occurred. The mass of the wood is formed of a fine Quercus, resembling Q. glauca, it is a beautiful and a shady tree. Next to it in abundance is Rhododendron majus, now in full flower, and forming a beautiful object, Rhododendron minus ceases with the barrener tracts. Magnolia is very conspicuous, Pinus cedroides common towards the pagoda; Eurya not rare, Gaultheria nummulifolia continues throughout, Valeriana violifolia, Oxalis acetoselloides, Bryum, Butia purpurea, Sambucus, Saxifraga of Bulphai, and another species, Bambusa microphylla, Swertia, Luzula, Thibaudia orbicularis, Primula Stuartii, occurred between the commencement of the ascent and the pagoda; at between 7,300 to 7,600 feet, Magnolia odoratis.

At the pagoda and village, Pinus cedroides, P. pendula, Bambusa of Sanah, Mespilus microphyllus, Magnolia grandiflora, Berberis asiatica, Q. anthoxylia, Coriaria, Rosa altera of Bhoomlungtung, Elæagnus, Salix and Allium of Bulphai, occur.

Chindupjee is situated on a rivulet close to the confluence, with a larger stream. Around it, or at least between the village and the larger stream, picturesque patches of sward bordered with a very picturesque oak. Q. ilecifolia occur; this tree predominates all about the village, it is certainly the prettiest place we have yet seen.

2 *n*

Some cultivation occurs around, chiefly of barley, with a little portion of radishes. The valley is surrounded by comparatively low mountains, most of which are rather bare, many are transversely furrowed on the surface, this may arise from their having been at some former period under cultivation.—The prevailing trees on the surrounding heights are firs, Pinus pendula and cedroides. No fish are to be seen in the river. The birds are the raven, white-necked starling, *bull-finch*, crimson and yellow shrikelets, blue tomtits, lesser ditto with two stripes on the head, white-rumped waterchat, red-tailed chesnuty sparrow.

The plants are Q. ilecifolia, Magnolia grandiflora, Laurinea, Hamamelidioides, Castanea aromatica, Pinus cedroides and pendula, Bambusa microphylla, and B. of Sanah which may be a variety depending on its marshy sites, Rhododendron minus, Salix, Mespilus microphyllus, Gaultheria nummularoides, Elæagnus, Marchantia, Swertia, Rumex, Daphne papyracea, Dipsacus, Artemisia major, Berberis asiatica, Rosa hispida, Rubus cæsius, Stauntonia latifolia, Tofieldioid of Sanah and Pemee, Taxus, Mespilus microphyllus, Ilex dipyrena, Oxalis acetoselloid, Thymus, Lycopodium of Surureem, Juniperus.

Bamboos split and inverted, and then placed in the ground, are used to scare away beasts from the cornfields.

March 26*th*.—Left at seven and a half and proceeded along the river which runs by Chindupjee, the path running over the spurs of the hills, forming its right bank. After proceeding about four miles, we crossed the nullah, changing our direction, and proceeding up a tributary, until we reached a prettily situated, and rather large village, thence we commenced to ascend over naked slopes with intervening woods, until we reached the base of the chief ascent, which is not very steep, although of good length, chiefly over naked hills. On reaching the summit, which is about 10,000 feet high, we commenced to descend, and the descent continued uninterruptedly and steeply until we reached Rydang, where we halted.

We passed only one village, which is about five miles from Chindupjee, and of similar size, but we passed in the more elevated places two temporary ones, apparently intended for the residence of the herdsmen of yâks or chowry-tailed cows, as a herd of these animals was seen feeding near each place.

The march throughout was beautiful, in the more elevated and drier portions, winding over swardy slopes or through woods of fir trees: on the descent from 9,000 feet downwards, passing through beautiful forests, chiefly of oak, and diversified in every possible way. The long-tailed pie was met with in the first portion, about 7,800 feet, the speckled chatterers at 8,500 feet, red shrikelet at 7,800 feet, and a new hawk at 8,300 feet. I observed the water-ouzel again as high as 8,000 feet. The new plants were a Carex, 6,500 feet, a sileneous plant past flowering, from the *same* limestone formation.

At 7,800 feet, and not far from Chindupjee, Pinus spinulosa again re-appears, it becomes common towards the village alluded to, and continues throughout the ascent, up to 9,300 feet, P. cedroides was uncommon during the first part of the march, its place being occupied by P. spinulosa, afterwards it re-appeared, and continued abundant up to 9,300 feet, it re-appeared on the descent about the same elevation, and continued to about 8,000 feet. Abies densa commences at the base of the chief ascent: at 10,000 feet, it is the only fir to be seen, it descends but a short way on the Rydang side. In the higher portions it occurred mixed with a Juniper, which in proper places becomes a small but elegant tree.

At the village on 7,000 feet, observed Rosa hispida, Ligustrum of Jaisa, Philadelphus, Pinus spinulosa common, as also Pinus cedroides, Bambusa of Sanah very common. Near this, larks were heard soaring high above us.

At 8,500 feet, Pendulous lichens becoming plentiful, Lonicera villosa.

At 9,000 feet, Abies densa appears, Acer sterculium, Betula, Bogh Pata, Rhododendron fruticosa, foliis ellipticis basi cordatis.

At 9,300 feet, Abies densa common, P. cedroides rare, spinulosa 0, pendula 0, Rosa hispida, Gaultheria nummularioid, which as usual continued throughout, Hypnum scolopendroid, Sphagnum, Bogh Pata very common, Rhododendron foliis ellipticis basi cordatis subtus argenteis, which I found on the descent as low as 8,000 feet.

At 9,500 feet, Bogh Pata very common, trees covered with Pendulous lichens, Bambusa of Sanah, Abies densa everywhere.

At 10,000 feet, Abies densa, Juniperus, Rhododendron obovata, foliis subtus argenteis; I am not sure whether this, is a variety or not, but it indicates greater elevation than the ferruginous one Rhododendron gemmis, viscosis, foliis lanceolatis, supra venosis, subtus subargenteis very common, Gnaphalium, Mespilus microphyllus, Rosa hispida, Swertia, Berberis spathulata, Orthotuck, Cerastum inflatum, Hemiphragma, Bogh Pata, Primula globifera, Pedicularis Dicranum nigrescens, etc. Limonia, Laureah.

Daphne papyraceæ occurs at the same elevation, chiefly on the side of the descent. From this place an opening is visible to the north-west, occupied by low hills. Juniperus very fine occurs, Compositæ abundant. Snow lies in the hollows and sheltered woods.

At 9,600 feet, Lonicera villosa, Rosa microphylla, Buddlæa purpurescens! Berberis spathulata, Spiræa belloides, Hydrangea! Rhododendron foliis lanceolatis, etc. as above, forming thick woods, Abies densa, Bogh Pata, Bambusa, Limonia lanceolata.

At 9,400 feet, Prunella, Cerastium inflatum, Labiata spicata, Baptisia! High ground 14 to 15,000 feet, is seen forming a lofty heavily snowed ridge to the north.

At 9,000 feet, Pinus cedroides re-appears, Bogh Pata, Rhododendron as before, Daphne papyraceæ, Thibaudia orbicularis, Limonia lanceolata, Dalibarda, Polygonum rheum!

At 8,800 feet, Rhododendron hispida, Abies densa ceased, Limonia lanceolata common, Lonicera villosa, Rubus triphyllus, Acer! Taxus! Primula Stuartii! Rubia cordifolia!!

At 8,500 feet, Chimaphila, Rhododendron obovata-ferrugina! Pinus cedroides, here and there, of immense size, diameter of one-six feet, Lycopodium of Surureem, Bogh Pata, Gaultheria flexuosa, Q. ilecifolia, also a very large and tall tree.

At 8,400 feet, Taxus very common, Smilax gaultherifolia, Olea, Sarcococea very common, Thibaudia orbicularis, Laurinea, Hamameloides. Beautiful glades here occurred, trees covered with mosses: another fine oak, Q. castaneoides commences, Daphne papyraceæ very common, Composita penduliflora, Hemiphragma, Rhododendron elliptica, foliis basi cordatis subtus punctatis, Ilex! Berberis intermedia, Laurinea uniflora, large Umbellifera of Rodoole descent..

At 8,000 feet, Acer, Primula Stuartii, Rhododendron majus! R. argentea commences.

At 7,500 feet, Cedar ceased, Rhododendron majus very common, Taxus diminishing, Sphæropteris, Ericinia soloræfolia, Lomaria of Khegumpa, Thibaudia orbicularis ceases.

At 7,300 feet, Berberis pinnata, Spiræa bella, Cycnium, apple tree. Here we emerged on open space in front of a hill, on which several detached houses stood, around which Pinus pendula was very common. Barley cultivation. Several small villages visible around, and to the north, in front of the snowy ridge, a curious truncated mountain was seen, its apex covered with snow.

Magnolia! Conaria! Cycnium, Viburnum canescens! Gaultheria arborea, Berberis intermedia very common, Fragaria.

At 7,200 feet, Q. tomentosa! the others have ceased, Gaultheria fruticosa, Rhododendron arborea, minus and argentea, in fine flower, Eurya æcuminata, Smilax, Gaultherifolia, Thibaudia caudata, Q. robur, Gleichenia major, Salix as before, Artemisia major, Rumex, Valeriana violifola, Rosa, Berberis asiatica, Ervicia crucifera, Thlaspi, Callitriche, Calamus.

The curious features are, the absence of Thibaudia obovata on the descent, and of Mespilus microphyllus, the substitution of Thibaudia orbicularis, and its low descent, the abundance of Taxus, size of the cedar and Q. ilecifolia, the re-appearance at same elevation of Magnolia grandiflora, occurrence of Rubia cordifolia, at such an elevation, etc.

Rydang is prettily situated towards the bottom of a rather narrow valley. There is a good deal of barley cultivation about it. I also noticed Cycnium, Celopecurus, Acorus Calamus, Corydalis! Fragaria, Cardamina, Rosa, Berberis, Ilex, Plantago, Rumex, Viola, Artemisia major, Daphne papyraceæ, Gentiana pygmæa of Khegumpa, Houttuynia! Pomacea, Callitriche, Dipsacus, Berberis pinnata, Elæagnus, Q. robur, ilecifolia. Of birds the long-tailed pie! is common. Berberis asiatica, Viburnum, Caneun, apple, Quercus microcarpus, Orthodon, Pteris aquilina, Ophiopogon, Angustis, Valeriana violifolia, Urtica urentium, Stellaria media, Eurya acuminata, Betula.

March 27th.—Our march commenced with a steep descent to the Gnee, a river of average size. We then continued descending along it for sometime, crossing it once on our way: we then diverged up a small nullah, and then commenced a very steep ascent, of about 2,000 feet. ·After attaining this, we proceeded through woods, or over sward at about the same elevation, still continuing along the Gnee. We subsequently commenced to descend at first through fine oak woods, then over barren naked hills. We reached Santagoung, about three and a half miles distance in a direct line, but fourteen miles by the road, highest point traversed 8,000 feet; lowest reached 6,000.

During first part of descent, noticed one or two straggling cedars and Taxus, Primula Stuartii, the woods were formed by Quercus robur, tomentosa, Gaultheria arborea, Rhododendron minus, Scabiosa re-appears, Clematis nova species, Sambucus, Rubus cresius, Composita pendulifolia, etc. as at Rydang.

Along the Gnee, the beech became plentiful, as also two Viburnums, both trees, together with the Cupulifera of Tongsa was here common and in fine foliage. Juglans, Incerta of Boodoo, Gaultheria, Mimosa arborea, Cupressus pendula, Conaria, Berberis racemosa and pinnata, Quercus microcarpus, Woodwardia, Thibaudia myrtifolia, Marlea! Cucurbitaceæ menispermoides, Alnus of Beesa, Polygonium rheoides, Mespilus microphyllus! Gentiana pygmæa, Salix, Pyrus. The birds were the usual water birds, viz. ouzel, slaty-white rump, slaty-red tail, white-pated chat.

On the smaller nullah Bucklandia, Viburnum microphyllum, Bucklandia!

The ascent was at first through dry woods of Rhododendron minus, Q. tomentosa, Gaultheria arborea, a Taxus or two occurred at 7,000 feet, Indigofera cana, Rosa, Gaultheria fruticosa of Sanah aristatum.

At 7,000 feet, the same vegetation continued, Rhododendron minus very common, Pendulous lichens commencing.

At this elevation, in more moist spots, woods thick, differently constituted, Quercus glauescense, Castaneoides ilecifolia, here and there Rhododendron majus, Magnolia grandiflora.

Gaultheria fluxuosa, Pinus cedroides rare, Vaccinium cyaneum, Rosa hispida! Saxifraga! Thibaudia orbicularis and caudata, Mespilus microphyllus, Azalea, Ilex, Symplocos, Tussalago of Churra, Acer, Thibaudia obovata, Pendulous mosses abundant.

The remainder of the vegetation afforded little of interest; consisted of stunted oaks, Q. tomentosa, Gaultheria arborea, Rhododendron minus: Serissoides reappears near Santagoung, Pinus longifolia, plantains.

The valley to the left towards Santagoung is on the left side well populated and cultivated.

March 28th.—Santagoung, a small village 6,300 feet above the sea, situated on bare hills, between two loftier ridges. Country around well inhabited and well cultivated in the terrace style: villages numerous. Pinus longifolia, Rosa, Azalea, etc. occur here as before. A lake or jheel was observed 500 feet, below the village of some extent, formed in a natural hollow, abounding with Scirpus trigueter of Churra, and Hydropeltis. Water-fowl, snipe, and red pie-like peewit or plover.

The march commenced with a steep descent, which continued until we reached the river.

Crossing this we ascended 1,000 feet, and then proceeded in an undulating manner over naked hills until we reached Thain, distance six miles; the greatest descent was about 1,800 feet, ascent 1,000 feet; the country naked; no forest. The hills for some extent towards Thain appeared from some cause very red.

But little interesting vegetation occurred: noticed a huge Cupressus pendula, half-way to the Gnee. Vegetation otherwise much the same as towards Tassgong, Valeriana violæfolia, Azalea, Campanula linearis, Rubus deltoides, Aspidium macroser., Artemisia major, Pinus longifolia straggling, only plentiful near Thain, Anthistiria minor! Primula Stuartii, Mimulus, Gentiana pumila, Alnus, Flemingia secunda, Morus rubeseoides, Salix, Quercus, Viburnum microphyllum.

At the river Cæsalpinia . Ficus obliqua! Desmodium, Salix, Indigofera cana, Arundo, Luculia.

On the ascent Holcus, Elæagnus, Santalacea, Clematis cana, Senecionoides, Conyza vulgaris, Emblica, Schænanthus, Phyllanthus ruber, Q. tomentosa, Desmodium vestilum, Briedleia obovata! Nerium canum, Euphorbia antiquorum, Jasminum of Benka, Ligustrum conaria, Mesp. microphyllus (are these two species confounded by me, as the larger-leaved one never descends so low?), Lerissoides, Osbeckia linearis, Euphorbia, Gordonia, Gymnobotrys. Red-legged crow; in descent altitude 5,800 feet, the most common plant is a species of Berberis very nearly allied to B. asiatica. Rain in the afternoon.

March 29th.—Mimulus, Acorus Calamus, Quercus robur, Rhododendron minus, P. longifolia, Gymnobotrys, Campanula linearifolia, Rosa tetrapetala, Gordonia, Salix, Verbena officinalis, majus, rugus, Lemna, Gentiana, Hypericum japonica, Indigofera cana, Schænanthus, Senecio, Buddlea of Nulka, Pyrus, wheat, Ervum, Vicia, Potentilla, Q. tomentosa, Cypressus, Ficus, Berberis, Phyllanthus ruber.

Blackbird, sparrow-hawk, and Hoopoe about houses; it has a curious hoop, varied with a grating chirp.

The blackbird frequents houses here; its voice is very discordant and singular, sparrow-hawks were seen to pursue wounded pigeons. Houses few, built of unbaked and large bricks or rather cakes of mud. The village of Wandipore is visible to the south-west, about one and a half mile. Snow on ridges to west, all which are lofty. The country around Wandipore is tolerably populous, though not so much so as about Santagoung.

We were compelled to halt at Phain or Thain, until the 1st instant, owing to the admirable management of the Bhooteas. It appeared at first as if the Zoompoor or Governor of Wandipore was determined that we should not be gainers in time by not going through his castle, but subsequently it turned out that the Deb had, with infinite consideration, wished us to remain in order to rest ourselves after our long journey. This may have been merely said to shelter the Wandipore man, who had the impudence to send one evening to us saying, that the Deb and Durmah were coming to Wandipore next morning, and that we were to meet them there, and return the same evening to Punukha. This turned out untrue. Pemberton was at last compelled to write to the Deb, and the consequence was the arrangement for our advance next morning.

April 1st.—The march to Punukha extended over a most barren dried up country, the features presented were the same as those about Phain. We proceeded at first in the direction of Wandipore, then diverged, proceeding downwards in the direction of the villages. The remainder of our journey extended either just above the base of the hills, or along the valley: the distance was nine miles. The march was an uninteresting one; the only pretty part being the river that drains the valley, and it is one of considerable size, fordable in but few places; the rapids are frequent, but the intermediate parts flow gently. We were all dreadfully disappointed in the capital, the castle even is by no means so imposing as that of Tongsa or Byagur; the *city* miserable, consisting of a few mean houses, and about as many ruined ones.

The surrounding cultivation is chiefly poor wheat; the hills the most barren conceivable. On arriving near the palace we made a detour, to avoid exposure to the usual regal insolence: our plan was effectual. From some distance I had espied our quarters, and although our mission, is one sent by the most powerful eastern government, yet we had allotted to us a residence fit only for hogs.

It consisted of a court-yard, surrounded by walls, and what had evidently been stabling; the apartments were numerous, but excessively small, the roof of single mats. The place swarmed with vermin. In this we determined not to stay, and so proceeded to the city, (for sure there cannot be a capital without a city,) and there, after some delay, procured two houses, in one of which the present Tongso Pillo had lodged before his present exaltation. But imagine not that it was a palace. The two houses together furnished three habitable rooms.

I imagine not that the houses were procured for us by the local government. We only obtained them by Pemberton's liberality was well known. The Sepoys' lines were transported hither not by Bhooteas but by our own people. In addition the people are in many cases insolent, and it was only after a peremptory message to the Deb, stating what the consequences would be of such a system of annoyance, that we got any assistance.

April 3rd.—We have heard nothing of the Mutaguat. It appears that the country is unsettled now. The old Deb having possession of Tassisudon, and the people here declaring they will stop all supplies if the Deb does not, according to custom, repair at the usual period to Tassisudon. A Deewan here, who has held office under four Rajahs, says, that the present truce is owing to the hot weather; Bhooteas only admire fighting in the cold season, in conformation of which, he says that in the cold season the contest will be renewed. There will then be an additional bone of contention for the present. Nor should I much wonder if the Paro Pillo then comes forward and takes the Debship and all away. The Deewan's account of the past fighting, places the Bhooteas in a most contemptible light: it appears that when they fire a gun, they take no aim, their only aim being to place their bodies as far as possible from the weapon; the deadly discharge is followed up by the deadlier discharge of a stone. At plunder they are more adroit.

The following plants may be found about this place; Ligustrum, Salex pendula, Valeriana orolifolia, Campanula linearis, senecionideæ, Viola, Jasminum, Rosea, Conaria, mangoe one tree in the gardens, Citrus two or three species in ditto, Jubrung, Diospyros, Acorus, Veronica, Ranunculus, Sclerossophalos, Alopecercus, Agrostides, Bombax, stunted weeping cypress; Pinus longifolia, Punica, Dipsacus, Potentilla, Potamogeton 2, Hyperia japonica, Lysimachia, Chenopod. Ajuga, Anisomales.

Birds—great kingfisher, diver snappet, white-pated rumped chats, no ouzels. Part of the gardens extend from the palace up the river to the village; the breadth is fifty to seventy yards, the length 200. They are surrounded by a dilapidated stone fence. Although an Assam malee or gardner resides in them, they are kept in miserable order: the soil seems good, the trees flourishing, mangoe, Diospyros, Jubrung, oranges, citrons, pomegranates, are the principal trees. The south side has a streamlet running along it outside the fence, for the supply of water. This streamlet abounds with Acorus Calamus.

April 9th.—Our interview with the Deb took place. We dismounted at the boards over the streamlets above mentioned. and then

2 o

proceeded over the wooden bridge across the Patcheen, which is here a wide and deep stream: the bridge was partially lined with guards, in different dresses, few in uniform; it was besides armed with shoulder wall-pieces, capital things for demolishing friends. We then crossed a sort of court-yard and then ascended a steep and extraordinarily bad flight of steps to the door of the palace. Here we found the household troops all dressed in scarlet with two door-keepers, one seated on either side of the door: this led us into a quadrangle. The citadel being in front, the side walls were rather low, although viewed externally they appear of good height, but the ground of the interior is much raised. We crossed this diagonally, passed into the opposite quadrangle on the west side, and thence ascended into a gallery, hung with arms, and filled with followers, from this we passed after a little delay into the Rajah's room.

This was handsomely decorated with scarfs, the pillars were variously ornamented. The Rajah was seated on an elevated place in the corner, and appeared a good-looking well-bred man. He received the Governor General's letter from P. with much respect, getting up from his chair: the visit was a short one, and entirely of ceremony. The presents were deposited on a raised bench in his front. Communications were kept up by the Deewan and the Zimpay, formerly Joongar Zoompoor or Governor. On retiring we were presented with fruits, oranges, walnuts, horrid plantains, ghee, eggs and rice.

The whole business went off very well, no attempt at insolence. The concourse of people was greater than I expected. Swarms of Gylongs, the more curious of whom received whacks from leathern straps, wielded by some magisterial brother.

April 10th.—Yesterday we saw the Dhurma, to whom we had to ascend by several flight of steps, which are most break-neck things, the steps overlapping in front, and being often lined with iron on the part most subject to be worn. We found him in the south room of the upper story of the citadel. We waived our right to sitting in his presence as the question was put to us with respect and delicacy. The Rajah is a good looking boy, of eight or ten years old: he was seated in the centre, but in an obscure part of the room, and was not surrounded by many immediate attendants. The balcony was filled with scribes with handsome black, gilt, lettered books before them. Two other scribes were likewise engaged on our right, noting down what passed, but they seemed to be very bad writers. The visit went off well. The room was tastily, but not so profusely ornamented with scarfs as was the Deb's.

On returning we found the household guard drawn up in front to prevent our passing out without paying a fee. This matter was soon settled forcibly, and the durwan, or door-keeper, lost by his impudence the present he would otherwise have had from P., besides being in a great fright lest the affair should be reported to the Rajah.

April 11th.—The rains appear to have set in: the sky is constantly over-cast, and showers are by no means unfrequent. One of our dawks arrived opened: this no doubt took place in the palace, although the Deb strenuously denies it. Messengers are to be sent to Tassgoung, where the accident is said to have happened. The cause of its having been opened, is no doubt the report that there was a letter in it from the old Deb.

April 14th.—A violent squall unaccompanied by rain, came on yesterday from the west: roofs were flying about in every direction, and many accidents occurred from the falling of the stones by which they were secured. Part of the palace was unroofed. The storm has stopped all our amusements, particularly as the Gylongs attribute it to our firing. The Kacharies, our servants, were likewise requested not to play any more on the esplanade. This is just as it has been in every other place in Bootan, nothing is said against amusement until the presents have been received, and then we are requested to do nothing, and the authorities become disobliging!

The potters fashion their earthernware entirely with their hands, the upper half is finished on a flat board; the lower being added afterwards; the finishing is done chiefly by a wet rag, the operator revolving around the pot. The vessels chiefly used for carrying water are oval, these are covered with black glaze.

Some Didymocarpi very fragrant, one near Chindupjee most grateful, resembling quince and sandal wood; the odour is permanent, and appears to reside in the young leaves before their expansion: Iris, Hypericum, Viola, Ligust., Ranunculus, Verbasena, Gymnostomum, Serratula arenaria, Veronica.

CHAPTER XIII.

Return of the Mission from Bootan.

May 9th, 1838.—We left Punukha at twelve, having been delayed throughout the morning, on account of coolies. We crossed the palace precints, and the two bridges unmolested. Our road lay in the direction of our entering Punukha for sometime, but on the opposite bank of the river. We gradually descended throughout this portion. Then at about eight miles turning round a ridge, we followed a ravine to the west, some distance above its base, gradually descending to the watercourse draining it. Thence we ascended in a very circuitous route to Telagoung, the castle of which is in a ruinous state: it is visible from the place whence one turns to the westward.

Up to this point, which was certainly 1,200 feet above Punukha, no change occurred in the vegetation. The country remained barren, the ravines in favourable places being clothed with underwood, and as we increased our elevation, with trees. Noticed a Bupleurum, Viburnium sp., Ficus obliqua.

At 3,500 feet, Sambucus, Bupleurum sp., Potentilla as before, Gentiana pinnata, Serissoides, Campanula.

At 3,800 to 4,000 feet, Pinus longifolia more common though still a stunted tree, Emblica, Pæderia cyaneum, Q. tomentosa, Primula Stuartii, Parochetus, Pogonantherum, this is a most common grass about here, it becomes more stunted as we proceed lower, and its extreme elevation does not exceed 6,000 feet, Acorus very common, Adhatoda!

At 4,000 feet, Simool, Dipsacus as before, Aspidium, Macrodon, Rhododendron minus re-appears.

On rounding the ridge, although we did not increase our elevation, the country became more wooded. In some places Q. robur, Gordonia, Pyrus were common, others and the greater portion were composed of Pinus longifolia, Bucklandia re-appears at 4,500 feet, Azalea, Saccharum aristatum, Hedera, Didymocarpus contortus, on rocks.

Towards the nullah we passed a village with some wheat and buckwheat cultivation ; Plantago, Ranunculus, Thymus, were interspersed. Along the watercourse Symplocos styracifolius, which becomes a middling-sized tree, was seen, and Stellaria cana, petalis albis profunda partitus, as well as S. media.

Our section was as follows :—

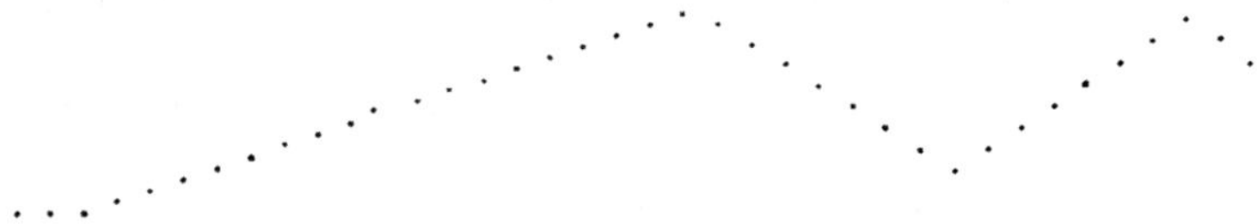

Telagoung is a middling-sized, dilapidated castle, in which it is settled the first blood is to be shed in the forthcoming contest, it is occupied by the old Deb's men. Up to its walls, thickets abound, and the fragrant rose was very conspicuous.

Its elevation is about 5,600 feet, yet a Ficus may be seen planted by the side of Cupressus pendula, and Punica thrives. The change in temperature was very great. Birds abounded throughout ; a new sombre-coloured dove was shot by P. : the most common birds were the orange-billed shrike of towards Tumashoo.

May 10th.—We left Telagoung at 7 A. M. and descended instantly to a small nullah, from which we re-ascended. The ascent continued without intermission, occasionally gradually, but generally rather steep for three or four hours. The descent occupied about as long, and about three-fifths the distance, following nearly throughout a small nullah. Woollakkoo, our halting place, is a good-sized village, and fourteen and a half miles from Telagoung.

To the nullah I observed Stellaria cana, Berberis asiatica, which has re-appeared, Erythrina, Rubus deltoid, which is very common all over these parts and whose fruit is palatable, Uvularia, Swertia plantaginifolia, Cæsalpinia, Mimulus, and Urtica foliis apice erosis.

The ascent commenced through woods of Q. robur, the shrubs consisting of Gaultheria fragrans and arborea, a Myrsinea, Thibaudia serrata, whose inferior limit is here, Rhododendron minus, but not very common. A good deal of wheat cultivation and of better quality occurred at 6,500 feet, assuming Telagoung as 5,600 feet, Pteris aquilina common throughout and up to 10,000 feet.

At 8,000 feet, Taxus re-appears, with Baptisia in flower, Thibaudia orbicularis, Luzula of Chindupjee, Smilax gaultherifolia, Thibaudia obovata, Fragaria vesca, which continues throughout, and has a range of between 3 to 10,000 feet, Bambusa microphylla, and Acer sterculiacea appear, woods of Q. ilecifolia, up to 7,200 feet, chiefly of Q. robur, Gaultheriæ two common ones, occur commonly.

At 8,500 feet, the woods composed chiefly of Q. castaneoides and glaucum, Q. ilecifolia less common. No Q. robur, path-like glades and rather open, Pythonium ecaudata, up to 9,000 feet, Primula pulcherrima very common.

At 8,500 feet, Saxifraga of Khegumpa and of Chindupjee, Mitella! Luzula, Carex, Viola reniformis, Lomaria of Khegumpa, Hedera, Ilex, Mercurialis, grey lichens.

Taxus, Quercus, Rhododendron, another species foliis subtus ferrugineo-argenteis floribus rosaceis.

Smilacina, Ophiopogon, Urtica carnosa decumbens, Limonia laureola, Pythonium ecaudatum.

At the same elevation and indeed below us, but on other ridges, cedars were seen in abundance: Hydrangea and Hydrangeacea calyptrata, Epilobium sp. withered.

At 7,800 feet, Aristolochia novum genus, Tritium glaucum, Thlaspi, Arabis cordata, Loranthus, Symplocos sessiliflora.

At 7,900 feet, Lardizabalea.

At 8,000 feet, Hamiltonia?

At 9,000 feet, Crucifera floribus amplis albis, on mossy banks, with Mitella, Spiræa densa.

Acer sterculiacea in forests, Cerasi sp. common.

Betula, Ribes, Arenaria, Lilium giganteum, Laurinea, Chimaphila, Acer.

At 9,300 feet, Rhododendron hispida and rosaceum, Taxus, Pythonium filiformia, Trillium album, Salvia of Royle, Rhododendron ferrugineo and obovata, Smilacinia densiflora, Sarcococea, Daphne cannabinum, here in flower, Anemone, Prunella, Hemiphragma, Cedar, but rare.

At 9,700 feet, Primula Stuartii in flower lower down, but here quite past, Corydalis linetta, Viola, Juniperus, Viburnum floribus magnis albis, Rhododendron deflexa, in flower. Acer: 1, vel. 2, Cerasi sp. altera, Paris polyphylla, and from 7,000 feet, Iris foliis angustis, Cerasus apetalus gathered below here a shrub, very common, Osmundia alia, Berberis ilecifolia and integrifolia, Rosa microphylla, Spinis latis, Baptisia, Corydalis altior floribus luteis, Aconiti sp., Papaveracea succo aqueo, ferrugineo hispida, capsula siliquosa, 3-valvis, replis totidem, stigmata radiata, 5-lobo. Prunella, Betula, Ranunculus minimus, Carex, Mimulus! Sambucus of below, Salvia of Royle. Polytrichum rubescens.

From the ridge the view to the south is pretty, the country undulated, either naked and swardy, or clothed with firs.

Abies spinulosa commences: and is soon succeeded by Pinus pendula, which, as we proceeded lower, soon became the chief tree; Rhododendron obovata finely in flower, Lilium giganteum common Trillium atratum, Ribes lacineat.

Q. ilecifolia re-appears 500 or 600 feet below the ridge, Pinus spinulosa common, with a Salix, grey pendulous lichens.

At 6,000 feet, P. pendula, Mespilus microphyllus, Larix, Rumex, which has occurred throughout, Salvia alia viscosa foliis subhastatis trilobis, Cycnium, Astragaloides! bracteis subvaginant magnis, Rosa latispina becomes very common.

At 8,800 feet, Hedera, Hamiltonia re-appears, Galium sp., Juncus, Oxlip, Clematis, Salix, very common.

At 8,500 feet, a village is seen to the right; Q. ilecifolia is the chief tree, with P. pendula, Azalea, Baptisia, Pomacea of Rydang, Rhododendron arbor. minus. Red-legged crow, pine chatterers.

At 8,000 feet, Baptisia continues; all alpine vegetation ceased; Rhododendron minus continues, Q. ilecifolia, but no Corydalis, Anemone, Iris, etc. although Oxlip does; Salix continues.

The descent to the halting place is marked by return to the old vegetation indicated by re-appearance of Elæagnus fragrans and Rosa tetrapetala, Valeriana violifolia.

Baptisia rotundifolia and oblonga, this last a tree very common, Pinus pendula chief tree, Pomacea celastufolia, Elæagnus fragrans, Rosa tetrapetala, very common along the nullah, Baptisia continues low down, as Oxlip, Stauntonia alba, Viburnum, *Asteroides*, Jasminum luteum, Tussilago, Spiræa bella, found about the level of this.

All the monocotyledons have a defined elevation; Smilacina cordifolia is the lowest, except Uvularia, Lilacineæ and Trillium, are the highest, not being found much under 10,000 feet. There is an Osmundia likewise on the ridge, the fronds below are not contracted, it is ferrugineo-tomentosa. Hemiphragma has a wide range, between 6 and 10,000 feet: Salvia nubigena of Royle, confined to 10,000 feet, Aconitum, Corydalis lutea, lenella and cærulea, Prunus penduliflora, Papaveracea, Juniperus, Rhododendron obovata, Silacinea, Cerasus apetala, Ribes 2, are sure signs of elevation.

If the Mimulus be the same as that from Punukha, it has a very wide range, as also Lilium giganteum. Pythonium filiformeis, limited, as well as ecaudata, Crucifera, Anemone, Laurinea, Polytrichium, were all definite. Mitella ranges between 9 and 9,500 feet, it is strange that the chief variety in vegetation occurred on the Telagoung side, on which springs are rare. No Thibaudias occurred on the other side, Euphorbia was confined to the Woollakkoo side, as also Primula, etc. etc. The chief cultivation about Woollakkoo is of wheat, but from the mode of cultivation the plant is evidently adapted for irrigation ; rice is also cultivated. This is perhaps its maximum height. The hills around are covered here and there with snow, and must therefore be above 10,000 feet high. The highest were to the north-west.

The river is of moderate size, fordable in most places, but still well supplied with wooden bridges. Fish, in shoals too, were seen here and there.

May 11*th*.—Our march continued down this river throughout : we left its banks once or twice owing to ascending some hundred feet above its bed, occasionally it spread out, but generally was confined between the rocks. Its banks in some places were planted with weeping willows. The vegetation throughout was much the same. The most common plants were Rosa, this literally abounds, Pinus pendula, Viburnum grandiflora, a Symphoria ! Cratægus 2 species, Mespilus microphyllus, Lantoneă, Jasminum luteum, Berberis asiatica and obovata, Plectranthus canus, Elæagnus fragrans, Stellaria cana, Colquhounia, *Indigofera* sp. altera, Baptisia did not re-appear, Euphorbia continues, as does the Celastrus noticed yesterday, which commences at 8,500 feet.

Cycnium re-appears, it is in fruit, the cotyledons are not conduplicate. In the fields Stachys, Potentilla (common), Brumus, Lamium of Khegumpa, Cynoglossum, Thlaspi, Datura in waste places, Conaria, rare, Imperata ! Scabiosa of Bulphai.

A low shrub abounded on the road sides and walls, having all the characters of Plumbago, a Lantonea likewise abounded, Fragaria, Swertia, Taxaxacum, Cardamina lilacina, Herminu sp., Marchantia, Astragalus, Ranunculus, Carex, Potentilla supina, Potamogeton, Clematis grata, Poplars were seen ; of these, Taxaxacum very common. Quercus robur re-appears towards Lamnoo, as well as Juglans and Populus.

Weeping cypresses about villages, Hordeum hexastichum is commonly cultivated, A. Buddlæa floribus lilacinis noticed yesterday was found, its range is 8,500 to 7,500 feet, Zanthoxyla here.

A cuckoo was shot ; this bird would seem to be as in Europe attended by the Yunx, at least a cry very similar to that of that bird was heard. Lysimachia of Punukha, Campanula re-appears.

The most common bird is Lanuis. The sombre-coloured dove too is rather common. The wheat cultivated here is poor, a good deal of the Bromus occurs with it. Astragalus is common on the borders of the fields, and in some of them Ervum, Lamium and Vicia.

The whole upper surface of the column of Aristolochia of Telagoung, is viscid and stigmatic, and likewise the margins of the depressions in which the anthers are lodged, it is certainly akin to Rafflesiaceæ.

May 12*th*.—Proceeded to Chupcha, our march to, and indeed beyond Panga, seven miles from Lamnoo, was through exactly similar country. The hills naked or clothed with firs, the path lay along the river Teemboo chiefly, but occasionally we met with one or two stiff ascents. On reaching Panga it was determined to push on to Chupcha, which was said to be but a short way off; we started, and descended after sometime to the river, above which Panga is elevated about 1,000 feet. We continued along the river, until we commenced to ascend towards Chupcha, this ascent was very long and rather steep, the road tolerably good. We found Chupcha to be ten miles from Panga, and 8,000 feet high, the greatest height we crossed being 8,600 feet, and this day we were told, that all our climbings had ceased. The road was generally bad, and well furnished with rocks: in one place we passed from 100 yards along the perpendicular face of a cliff, the Teemboo roaring underneath, the road was built up with slippery slabs of stone. The country was generally very pretty, the scenery along the river being very picturesque. We passed a waterfall of considerable size, which is Turner's Minzapeeza. After leaving Panga we came on an uninhabited country, nor did we see more than one village, until we reached the ridge immediately above Chupcha, 1,000 feet above this, there is a very large village inhabited by Gylongs, the bare summit of the hill rising an equal height above it: snow visible to the south. The greatest distance we descended was 6,500 feet, the greatest height 8,500 feet. The distance seventeen miles, the longest march we have yet had.

The vegetation was nearly the same up to the time we turned off towards Chupcha, it was characterized by a profusion of Rosa, among which the Cratæga, Symphorema, (which is less common than towards Woollakkoo,) Rhamnus, Viburnum grandiflorum, Pinus pendula, Thymus, Cycnium.

In grassy banks of fields between Panga and Lamnoo, Astragalus, Ervum, Vicia, Aster major, Rumex, Agrostia, in fields Hieraciæ sp., Caricia sp., Lactuca, Bromus.

2 *p*

Salix pendula about villages. After leaving Panga we came on to a place called Minzapeeza, here Adiantum, Aspidium? Hamamelidea, Cedrela? Rhus, Galium, Tussilago, Saxifraga ligularis, Valeriana violifolia, Smilax flexuosa, Aruncus, Sarcococea, Azalea.

Rhododendron minus recommenced after leaving the river towards Panga, a straggling cedar or two occurred, Populus rotundifol. very common, Gaultheria arborea.

About Panga, Lithospermum, Oxalis corniculata, Umbellifera, from the flowers of which *moud* is made, Rubus, Arabis, Taxacum, Dipsacus.

Beyond the waterfall the Quercus robur became common, forming beautiful woods, it continued throughout until we re-descended to the river, range 7 to 7,500 feet. In these woods formed likewise by Pinus pendula, Convallaria cirrhosa appeared, Rubia cordifolia, hispida, Paris polyphylla, Aralia cissifolia, Mitella, Ribes! Spiræa, Asparagus, Epipactis, Avularia, Houttuynia! Arum viviparum on rocks, Duchesmium, Populus oblonga occurred also, Coriaria! Hedera common, Benthamia common.

On rocks along the river, Peperomia, 4-phylla, Populus oblonga, Acer sterculiacea! Symphoria alia! Indigofera, Salix, Cedrela, Sassafras, arbor facie, Gordonia, Vitis, Syringa, Serissa, Buddlæa, Sedum on rocks, Eriophon ditto, Campanula cana, Pinus pendula, Rosa, Convallarium cirrhosa, Polygonum robustum, foliis cordatis.

The ascent up to 7,500 feet, was marked by similar vegetation: up to this point the prevailing shrubs gradually disappeared, they were never so common as about Panga. Quercus robur having ceased, was succeeded by Quercus ferriuginea, which is much like Quercus ilecifolia, and has very coriaceous leaves, this again at 7,500 feet, was succeeded by Quercus ilecifolia, Dipsacus up to this, Pteris aquilina, Gaultheria arborea.

At 7,600 feet, Rhododendron oblonga, a most beautiful species, Calyce discoideo commenced, as also Rhodora deflexa and Rhodoracea ochrolenea, which is, I think, that I before noticed as R. elliptica, foliis basi cordatis subtus argenteis et punctatis, Euphorbia occurs also here, as also the Rosa, Berberis asiatica.

At 8,000 feet, the trees were covered with grey lichens, and assumed the usual highly picturesque appearance: noticed Primula Stuartii in flower (Symphoria! ceased), Euphorbia, Gaultheria nummularifolia commences, Artemisia major, Cratægus odoratus continues, Saxifraga ligularis common up to this, Ribes commences,

Gaultheria of Bulphai, Galum, Hyperici sp., Lilium giganteum, Clematis grata, Populus species, do not ascend above this.

At 8,500 feet, Rhododendron minus, Rhododendron oblonga, ochroleucum, Coccineum appears, Ribes, Smilax sanguinea, Gaultheria of Bulphai very common, arborea stunted, Limonia major, Clematis grata! Rhododendron hispida, Potentilla, Pteris aquilina, Berberis asiatica, Mespilus microphyllus, Gnaphalium, Swertia, Viola, Patrinum! Elæagnus fragrans! Thymus, which ranges from 6 to 10,000 feet, Euphorbia, Pedicularis, Cycnii sp., Mimulus, Rhodora deflexa, Pinus pendula, Quercus ilecifolia, both stunted, Pteris aquilina.

The descent to the village was about 500 feet, Arenarium on rocks, Mimulus viola, Rumex, Juncus, Acorus veronica, Anagallis, Pythonium of Blake, Euphorbia, Pedicularis, Carex, Mespilus microphyllus: pine chatterers throughout, at least above 7,000 feet.

The summit, which was certainly 9,500 feet, was completely bare: Pinus pendula ascends a long way.

Chupcha—Hordeum hexastichor in beautiful order, the chief cultivation. Red-legged crow; larger dove. The form of the country traversed is as follows:—

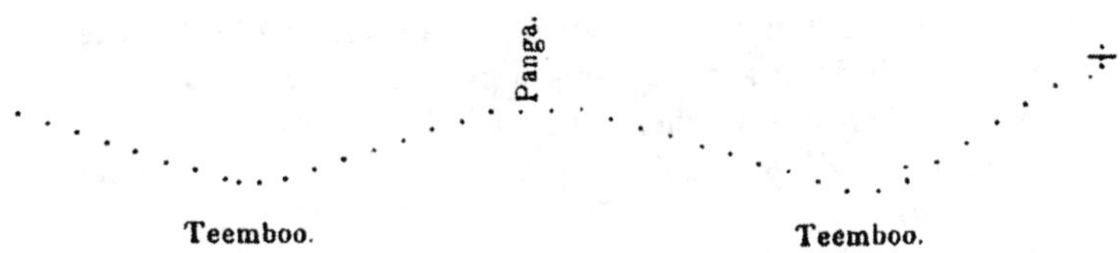

At Diglea we had an opportunity of seeing the mode of building in this part of Bootan; the houses are made of mud, which is trampled and beat down by men, who perform sundry strange evolutions while so employed; the mud is beat down in a frame-work; it is from the different layers formed that the lines seen outside finished houses result. The mode is slow, but must give great firmness.

May 14*th.*—Ascended to the Gylong village, above Chupcha, and then to the naked ridge. The village may be estimated as being 8,700 or 8,800 feet above the sea, and that part of the ridge to which I ascended as 9,800 or 10,000 feet. The ascent is uninterrupted up to the village; it winds through a fine fir wood, after diverging from the road to Panga, after that it is quite open, scarcely a shrub being met with until the ridge is surmounted. On turning to its northern face, woody vegetation becomes pretty abundant, and 500 feet below, woods occur. This is contrary to what usually happens; the south faces of mountains being supposed to be better wooded than the others, but in Bootan the difference would seem to be due to the piercing winds blowing from south, or up the ravine of the Teemboo. The scenery was very pretty, both in the woods before reaching the village, and from the ridge: vast quantities of snow visible to the north and north-east. I ascended to within 1,000 feet of snow, and I think that at this season, an elevation of 11,000 feet is required *in open places* to secure the presence of snow: it is obvious that local circumstances, such as shelter, etc. may cause it to descend nearly to 9,000 feet, and it is as obvious that snow will descend lower down a mountain of 15,000 feet high than one of 12,000; the difference in the beds of snow causing a greater reduction of temperature in the one than in the other. In an isolated mountain, an elevation of 11,000 feet will be required for the presence of snow in May.

At 8,000 feet, Baptisia, Viburnum canum, Umbellifera toxicaria, Colquhounia, Deutzia, the Symphoria of Teemboo.

At 8,200 feet, Salix, Abies spinulosa straggling, Rhododendron microphylla commences, the bruised has a terebenthaceous odour, Ilex, Gaultheria flexuosa, Parus major: variegated shortwing, Papilio machaonires.

At 8,300 feet, Saxifraga ligularis.

At 8,400 to 8,500 feet, Limonia, Viburnum grandiflorum or canum, Berberis asiatica, Mespilus microphyllus, Populus oblonga, Rhododendron ochrolena, Clematis grata viola lutea,* Epipactis, Hemiphragma.

At 8,700 feet, Rhododendron microphyllum very common, Ribes, Bupleuri sp.,* Rosa fructibus hispidis,* Rubia hispida, Sambucus, Berberis integrifolia, an vero distincta.

At 8,800 feet, Viola pusilla, Fragaria vesca and lutea, Baptisia, Rosa, Sphærostemma, Clematis grata, Pinus pendula, etc.

At 9,000 feet, commencement of sward, no trees, except stunted shrubs of Pinus pendula, Mespilus microphyllus, Baptisia, Gnaphalium

Pedicularis,* Rosa, Bistorta,* leaves with margins not united to the margins of pitchers of Nepenthes and Cephalotus, Pteris aquilina, Prunella, Rhododendron microphyllum, Euphorbia, Taxaxacum, Potentilla, Thymus, Primula Stuartii.

At 9,100 feet, Hyperica brachiata of Moflong.

At 9,300 feet, Morina Wallichiana, Osmundioid, Dipsacus, Scabiosa? capitulo nutanta, Verbascum, Juncus, Epilobia sp.

At 9,400 feet, Salix shrubby, Cyperus fuscescens of Tassangsee, dwarfed Larix.

At 9,500 feet, Anemona aurea commences, covering in some places the sward; it straggles down in favourable places with Iris angustifolia, to 9,300 feet, Primula Stuartii, Rhododendron microphyllum, Gnaphalia, Euphrasia.

At 9,800 feet, southern face of ridge bare, northern thickety, consisting of Rhododendron fruticosum, foliis ellipticis basi cordatis punctato lepidotis, Salix, Berberis, Pyrus aria, Bambusa, Tetranthera.

In wet sheltered spots, Iris angustifolia, Aconitum, foliis aconitoideum, on the sward Euphorbia radians. Below this a little, woods commence chiefly of Bogh Pata, Cerasus, Salix, Rosa fructibus hispidis, Acers, Abelia? Viburnum niveum, Hydrangea arbuscula, non-scandens, Berberis integrifolia. The woods are open, the open spaces occupied by remains of last summer's vegetation, as Compositæ, Umbelliferæ, Aquilegium, a plant five or six feet high, folii aconitoidie, etc. Epilobium.

Among these in the woods, Trillia sp., Saxifraga reniformis, Liliacea Brodidoid, Viola, Primula purpurea, a lovely species, Aconiti sp., Papaveracea hirsuta foliis, Aconitoid very common, Orchideæ, Ribes sanguina, Composita penduliflora, Arenaria pusilla of above Telagoung, Polygoni sp., pusilla repens hirsuit foliis cordata ovatis, vel reniformibus subtus purpurescent, Salvia nubicola? Euphorbia coccinea.

Abies densa appears, as also close to the Gylong village, from this elevation upwards, it is common.

Abies spinulosa common on north face at 9,000 feet, Abies pendula ascends on south side as high as 9,300 feet, but is stunted beyond 9,000 feet, it does not exist on north face.

Primula Stuartii throughout, very abundant.

The plants most limited were Papaveracea, Aconitum folium aconitoideum, Saxif. reniformis, Primula purpuria, Euphorbia radians. Rhododendron cereum, mentioned above, and another at 9,800 feet with similar leaves, but normal flowers, Abelia, Cerasus, Trillii sp., Anemona, Iris, Bistorta, Ribes, A. densa.

The most dispersed are Euphorbia coccinea, Salix, Bogh Pata, Mespilus microphyllus, Cyperus fuscus, Primula Stuartii, Rhododendron microphyllum.

Hordeum hexastichum gives fine produce here; nothing can exceed it in appearance, oats also occur mixed with it, but is not sown, at least, it occurs rarely on walls, Arabis, Magus stolonifer, Juglans in villages, (Ribes Juniperus in the Gylong village), Acorus, Carex, Stellaria cana, Media, Caltha, and Thlaspi.

The temperature is delightful, thermometer 46° at 7 A. M., 52° in the middle of the day.

May 15th—Left Chupcha for Chuka, distant seventeen miles. Our march commenced by a very steep and indeed almost precipitous descent to the nullah, at the foot of Chupcha, of 1,800 feet. Thence we ascended gradually until we reached a temple visible from Chupcha, at which place we returned to the course along the Teemboo. The remainder of the road undulating, varying in level from 6,000 to 6,500 feet, until we commenced the descent to Chuka, which was long and tedious: we reached this at 5½ P. M. The road latterly was very bad, we passed Punukha, a small village, about 300 feet below our path. The mountains closing in the Teemboo continue lofty, at least 9,000 feet. Iris, cedars, and Abies densa, were common on the loftier parts.

We passed some beautiful places, indeed the march throughout was pretty. The vegetation was beautiful, owing to the quantity of water on the road, a stream occupying each hollow, round many of which we wound. Glades and pieces of green sward were not uncommon.

The Lamium of Bulphai is found about Chupcha. On the descent to the nullah the following plants were found.

At 7,000 feet, Iris commences, with a species of Lychnis, ground bare and rocky, Umbellifera cana, Umb., from which *moud* is prepared, common.

At 6,800 feet, Quercus ferruginea commences, on rocks here Stemodium ruderalis, Lantonica of Panga, etc., Convallaria cirrhosa.

At 6,500 feet, Hedera common, Aristolochia tetrarima, Berberis obovata, Viburnum cærulescens, Filix ferrugineo tomentosa, Pteris dealbata.

Iris common to 6,500 feet, continues lower down, but scarce. Along the nullah, which is a middling-sized torrent, Rhus, Cederela toone, Acer sterculiacea, Hamamelis, Fici sp., scandens, Rhus, Juglandifolia! Populus oblonga, Sassafras, on the ascent to the temple, Populus of very large size, and the above trees. Fraxinus floribunda, Osmundia in profusion, Aristolochia tetrarima, Scabiosa, of Bulphai, Prunella, Fragaria vesca. Duchesnum, Sarcococea, Elæagnus fragrans, Galium of Panga cascade, Corydalis, which continues to Chuka, but is scarce below 5,000 feet, Deutzia, Lilium giganteum, Uvularia very common, Primula Stuartii, Woodwardia (scarce), Pythonium pallidium, Campanula cana, Panax herbacieæ 2 species, Rhododendron agaleoides of ridge above Chupcha, Buddlæa cana, Ranunculus of Taseeling, Benthamia, Anemona ranunculacea, Buxus, Delphinum sp.? common, Gaultheria nummularifolia, Jasminum lutium, Conaria. This ascent was about 500 feet. Long-tailed pie seen here, red-billed shrikelet, first met with towards Tumashoo, common now as far down as 4,500 feet.

On passing the temple, or rather before coming to it, we changed the vegetation which became of the ordinary *dry* character. Woods of Q. ferruginea mixed with Pinus pendula, Benthamia, Pteris aquilina, Viburnum cærulescens, Conaria, Polygonum of Teemboo, Rhododendron minus, Gaultheria arborea.

The remainder of the march consisted of a series of winding round spurs: at about an average elevation of 6,000 feet found a Pythonium foliis pedalis, spad. apice filiformo recurvo, vel erecto, spathe viridi, Didymocarpea odora contuso terebinthaceo, Solanum nigrum, Succulent urticeæ, Scabiosa of Bulphai, Gnaphalium, Polygonum globiferum, Scirpus eriophorus, Hippocratia angulata, Mitella, in damp spots, Cycnium, but rare, Sarcococea, Impatiens two species, one at 6,500 feet, with a creeping plant, foliis ranunculaceis floribus solitariis hypocrateriform albis. No Buxus or Delphinum was observed, in any other glens than the first crossed. Alnus became common soon, the pines disappeared, Osmundia common, Primula rotundifolia, Paris polyphylla, Bletia as of Churra at Punukha, Sphæropteris.

In some places Rhododendron minus common, and with it Quercus ferruginea, Rubia hirsuta, not uncommon throughout as far as 15,000 feet, Thalictroides majus, Houttuynia, Betula.

In glades, Smilax gaultherifolia, in a wood round the marsh a Pomaceous tree: on the march, Swertia, Peloria, Carex stricta, and of Chupcha, Spiranthes rubriflora, Berberis pinnata, Saxifraga of Bulphai occur here.

Still further on, the forest assumed the appearance of those towards Khegumpa. Q. robur, recommences, cedars straggle down;

Pinus pendula, more common, Arenariæ sp., Lomaria of Khegumpa, Hottoneoides ranunculofolia common, Luzula, Sedi sp., Sambucus common throughout in shady spots, Radsuræ sp., Daphne papyracea, rare, Acer sterculiacea common, Sabia, Hydrangencea calyptrata, Hamiltonia, this last common to 4,500 feet.

On wet rocks Hutchinsia, Arenaria, succulent Urticea. In woods Cucurbitacea cessifolia, Ajugæ sp., Polygonum rheoides. On open spots, Benthamium in flower, Gaultheria arborea, here of large size, pines cease without changing the elevation, Q. ferruginea ceased, this is limited to dry spots.

The first change indicated by the appearance of Laurineæ, and Symplocos among oaks and chesnuts. The woods continued thick for some time, but on commencing the descent, which is gradual, especially at first, Q. robur is common, Gaultheria arborea, Rhododendron minus.

At 5,500 feet Hottonia, Rubia hirsuta, Hydrangeacea calyptrata, Phytolacea, also at 6,500 feet, and as low as 4,000 feet, Senecio scandens, Verbenacea of Dgin appears, Uvularia, Duchesnia, Polygonum rheoides.

Umbellifera gigantea, Potentilla supina appear, Pythonium recurvum, Rhus, Dipsacus of Churra, Alnus, Pomacea macrophylla, Stauntonia angustifolia, Photinea parviflora, Benthamea disappears, in flower at least, Didymocarpea, Rhamnus, and also at 5,000 feet, Fragaria vesca, in fruit! Paris, Curculigo pygmæa appears, Sedum continues and ceases at 4,500 feet, Ranunculus of Taseeling found also as low as 3,600 feet, Daphne nutans appears. This found first near Taseeling, found as low as 4,000 feet, Primula Stuartii, Rhododendron minus, Viburnum cærulescens continue, Thibaudia myrtifolia, Rubus deltoideus appears.

At 4,500 feet, a Malvaceæ' Sidoides, Erythrina, Rosa fragrans, Pythonium sp. majus, spadicis apice filiformi 2-pedali, Incerta of Taseeling, Ribesioides, Quercus ferruginoides, Indigofera major, Berberis obovata, in fruit.

At 4,400 feet, Cuscuta, Hamiltonia, Hottoneoides, Daphne pendula vel nutans, Impatiens, Mimosa, Menispermum tropæolifolia, Celastrinia sp., Panax crucifolia, Hypericum japonicum.

At 4,300 feet, Conyza nivea, Q. robur, Indigofera major, of Tassgoung, etc. Gaultheria arborea, Hedychium appears! Buddlæa of Nulka, Mæsa salicifolia!

At 4,200 feet, Thibaudia lanceolata appears, ranges between 4,200 and 2,000 feet,. Sanicula, Cynoglossum, Zyziphi sp.

Along the bed of the river, Zizyphus arborea, Urtica, foliis apicæ erosis, Berberis obovata, Erythrina, Artemisia major, Elæagnus fragrans, and Stellaria cana, occur, the last ranges between 3 and 6,000 feet, Thlaspi, Polygonum globifera, Dendrobium pictum, Verbenacea of Dgin, Clematis, petiolis basi connatis demum induratus majus, Magnolia, Randia of Punukha, Liriodendron tulipif., Apocynum nerufolium.

At Chuka, Ficus elastica, but not flourishing, Musa, Salix pendula. Phytolacea, Buckwheat, Crucifera cordifructus, Sanicula, Stellaria cana, Thibaudia lanceolata, Cynoglossum, Vandea, Parkioides common.

The most limited plants are Iris, Silene, Aristolochia tetrarima vix infra 6,000 feet, Buxus, Delphinioid, Fraxinus non infra 6,000 feet, Epipactis ditto, Hutchinsia, Lomaria of Khegumpa, Mitella, Carex stricta of Chupcha, *Peloria*, Smilax gaultherifolia, Osmundia non infra 5,500 feet, Hydrangeacea ditto, Cucurbitacea cissifolia, found about Sudya, etc.

The most diffused, Hottonia, Q. robur, Gaultheria arborea, 5 to 3,500 feet, Corydalis.

The subtropical forms, Mimosa, Impatiens, occurrence of fleshy Urticea, Ficus elastica, but not flourishing, Musa, Salix pendula, Buckwheat, Urtica urens, peaches, Stellaria cana, Crucifera cordifructus, Panax curcifolia, Andropogon arbusculoid, Rubia cordata.

May 16*th*.—The fort of Chuka not being whitewashed, is not conspicuous : its situation is strong, and against Bhooteas would be impregnable. It occupies a low hill arising from the centre of the valley, one side of which is washed by the Teemboo or Tchien-chiw. The room we were lodged in was a good one. The village is a mean one, and consisting of three or four houses.

We crossed the river by a suspension bridge much inferior to that of Benka, and then rose gradually and inconsiderably, following the Teemboo. To this we subsequently descended by a most precipitous road built for the most part on the face of a huge cliff: we reached the Teemboo at its junction with a small torrent; the tongue of land here was strewn with huge rocks, and bore evidences of the power of the torrents, for it evidently had been once a hill, such as that we had just descended. Thence we continued ascending, following the river from which however we soon diverged to our right, but not far. The road was rugged beyond description. As we approached Murichom, it improved somewhat, but was still very bad

2 q

We reached this place which is visible for some distance at 5 P. M.; the march being one of eighteen miles. No villages occurred en route. The hills were densely wooded to the summits and much lowered in height than those to which we had been accustomed. Passed two waterfalls, one less high, but more voluminous than the other, is the Minzapeeza of Turner; both these occurred on the left bank of the river. Minzapeeza, is a fall of great height, but the body of water is small.

The vegetation to-day partook much of the subtropical character, almost all boreal plants being left behind. We ascended and descended between 3,000 to 4,500 feet near Chuka, Parkioides, Mimosa arborea! and M. frutex. Magnolia! Rubia munjista, Impatiens! Cucurbitacea!

Oxyspora latifola! Rosa fragrans, Incerta ribesioides, Piper! Urtica heterophylla! Wendlandia! Phytolacea, Daphne nutans, Rottleria! Curculigo orchediflora, Acer, Eurya pubescens, Rhus, Alnus! Adamia, Gordonia! Q. robur reappears at a lower elevation than before seen: Dipterocarpioides arbor vasta trunco ramoso! Smilax auriçulata! Pothos pinnatifid! Briedlia oblonga! Corydalis, Dipsacus, Acanthaceæ common, Rubiaceæ of a tropical character, such as Ophiorhizæ; Celastrus! Pythonium majus, Tetranthera macrophylla! Quercus coriacea! Gaultheria arborea scarce, Deutzia on the descent to the Teemboo, Macrocapnos, Sterculia platanifolia, Melica latifolia! Arundo! Achyranthes densa! Labiata spinosa of Khegumpa or Phlomis, Labiata, Quercoides. The rocks on the river side are covered with Epiphytical Orchideæ; Saurauja sterculifolia, Pythonium pallidum, Elæagnus fragrans.

Along the banks of the Teemboo, Pandanus! Rhododendron azaleoides, R. pulchrum, Lyellia, Begonia picta, Composita arborea! Ficus! on ascent above its banks, Dioscorea! Elæocarpus! Acrosticum atratum! Convallarium oppositifolia, Thibaudia loranthiflora! Pogostemon of Dgin! Leea! The only northern plant a species of Viola; Otochilus linearis! Entada! Kydia! Mussænda! Macrocapnos altera of Yen, Callicarpa arborea! Panax aculeato palmiformis supra decompositæ of Dgin! Solanum farinacium! Urena lobata! Marlea, Panicum plicatum! Before ascending to Murichom we made two descents to two streams, crossed by common wooden bridges: that nearer Murichom being the largest; elevation at 2,500 feet. Here tree-fern; Pythonium majus, Duchesnia, Lysimacha, Begonia of Punukha! Caryophyllea scandens, Urtica gigas! Modeceoides exembryonata! Commelina! Conbreta sp.! Bæhmeriæ! Piper spica caudata pendula and another species!! Euphorbia! Galina of Panga, Croton malvifolius! Bambusa major! Bauhinia! Engeldhaardtii!

Although we subsequently ascended 1500 feet, very little change occurred: no re-appearance of tropical forms, Sterculiacea novum of Moosmai, Adamia, Volkameria! serrata, Triumfetta mollis! Briedlia avalis of Chilleeri! Gortnera! Corydalis! Hydrangeacæ! Melastoma malabathrica!

The march was very tiresome, some of the ranges passed were high and well clothed with firs. Those marked thus* are subtropical or tropical, and one glance will show their predominance: only Corydalis straggles down. The woods were in many places damp, in others dry: it was obvious that less rain had fallen between Chupcha and Chuka, than in other situations: a large proportion of Laurineæ and Acanthaceæ appeared in the woods, with Gordonia: the oaks and chesnuts when they did present themselves bore a tropical form, pointed out by their coriaceous undivided or merely serrated leaves. I certainly never saw such a predominance of tropical forms, at such an elevation as 3,500 or 4,000 feet.

For Lyellia I had been hunting for three years, but never thought of looking for it at low elevations; as it was I believe given out to be a native of high places. Of birds, Bucco, Picus intermedius, green pigeon, azure shrikelet, occurred.

May 17*th.*—Murichom is a small village of eight or nine thatched: houses, it is well and prettily situated: about it maize and wheat are in cultivation, Ficus, Hoya, Dendrobium, Croton malvæfolius, Meliacea, Cedrela Toona, orange, Verbesina, Datura, Artemisia major, Echites, in fact it would be difficult to point out an elevational plant. The same remark applies to the march to Gygoogoo, distant twelve miles, and situated 500 feet below the road, but still it is about the same level as Murichom. The march commenced with a steep descent, followed by a steeper ascent, then winding along, in and out, at an average elevation of 5,000 feet. The road was very bad, rocky and rugged as usual, P. and B. passed the village, and pushed on to Buxa, a distance of twenty miles, which place they reached at 7 P. M. At Murichom, Ficus cordata, fructibus pyriformibus, Clerodendron infortunata, Adamia, Spilanthes, Melastoma malabathrica, Bignonia, Pentaptera. The Oollook or Simia Hylobates, of Upper Assam.

Scarcely any thing worth noticing occurred; the vegetation being precisely the same. No oaks or chesnuts, at least comparatively few:

Elæocarpus, Rhus, Gordonia are the most common trees; Pythonium common, Hoya rotundifolia. Gygoogoo, a small village of two or three houses, was passed.

May 18*th*.—Marched to Buxa, ascending from Gygoogoo over a wretched rocky road, winding in and out. No water was to be had until we reached a ridge from which to Buxa is one continued descent. This ridge is between 5 and 6,000 feet, and yet there is scarcely a change in the vegetation. Pythonium abounded, especially P. majus, which literally occurred in profusion. The trees towards the top of the ridge were covered with moss, but all appeared subtropical; a few chesnuts, E. spinosissima occurred, Bambusa nodosis, verticillatis, and spinosis.

En route thither, Pholidota imbricata, Thib. loranthiflora, Aralia terebinthacea, Rottleria foliis peltatis, Ranunculus of Taseeling, Meniscum majus, Byttneria ferox, Caladium foliis medio discoloratis sæpius atratis, Gnetum, Ixora, Choulmoogra, Phlogacanthi sp., Corisanthes of Sudya, Acer platanifolia, Croton foliis oblongis irregularis dentato-lobatis occurred before, between 2,500 to 3,500 feet, Calamus, wild plantains as before, Gordonia, Rhus, Mimosa, Rottleria, Wallichia, Sida cuneata, Tradescantia cordata, Æschynanthus fulgens, et altera, Tupistra, Lobelia baccifera, Costus, tree-fern, as high as 5,000 feet, Bambusa fasciculata; of birds, the large Bucco.

At 5,000 feet, Thibaudia serrata, and on this side, as low as 2,500 feet, myrtifolia, Gordonia, Pythonium majus and medium, cinnamon, Piper, Acer platanifolia, Mucuna, Angiopteris, Saurauja ferruginea.

At 5,300 feet, Polygonia pinnatifolia, Hookeria macrophylla, Aralia scandens, etc. as before.

On descent nothing remarkable, except steepness: same vegetation. Pythonium majus not below 3,000 feet, Guttiferæ at 3,000 feet, Acanthaceæ, Carduaceus 2,800 feet.

At 2,500 feet, Buchanania undulata, Hyalostemma undulatum, Roydsia.

What can be the cause of this tropical elevation at such altitudes? Buxa is hot enough for any tropical plants, as jacks, mangoes, Cactus, etc. are found in fine order. It is not attributable to a gradual rise, as the ascent from this to 5,500 feet, is excessively steep. It must be owing to local causes modifying the climate: at 5,000 feet on the Dgin route, there are many elevational plants, indeed more than of subtropical.

It must not be forgotten that no Pinus longifolia exists on this route after leaving Telagoung.

Buxa is a rather pretty place, but as usual poor: the Doompa's house is the only decent one in the place, the others amounting to eight or ten, are common huts. The big house occupies an elevation in the centre of the pass, being cut off from the neighbouring hill, on either side by a ravine, one of which is now quite dry, the other affords a scanty supply of water. The hills are covered with jungle, the only clearing being about Buxa, and this, except the flat summit of the hill, is overrun with bushes, Capparis modecea, Croton malvæfolia, Menisperma tropæolifolia, Bergeræ 2 species, Ixora, Brucea same as of the plains, Atriplex, Tournefortia of plains, Mæsa macrophylla, Mimosa scandens, Ficus elastica in good order, jacks, mangoes, oranges, plantains, Tabernamontana, Calamus, Cedrela Toona, are found.

Black pheasants, Bulbuls, Drongoles, Oorooa, Bucco, green pigeons. Long-tailed blue-crested shrike, etc. are found here. The Doompa, or Chong Soobah, is a man of no rank, and the place itself is of no importance, except as the pass or entrance between the mountains of Bootan and the plains of Bengal.

The descent from Buxa is gradual at first and not unpicturesque: after passing a small chokey about half a mile from Buxa, sandstone of a coarse nature commences. The descent is very steep, and continues so until within a short distance of a place called Minagoung, at which the bullocks are unladen at least of heavy baggage. The remaining descent is very gradual, and continues so for several miles. The march throughout and until the level of the plains is reached, was through tree jungle. The underwood being either scanty or consisting of grass.

On reaching the plains, the usual Assamese features presented themselves, viz. vast expanses of grass, intersected here and there with strips of jungle. Reached Chichacootta about 3 P. M.: distance eighteen miles, of which about fifteen were over either level or very gradually sloping ground. No villages occurred, and only one path struck off from the Buxa one. We passed two or three halting places.

The vegetation throughout was subtropical At the same elevation as Buxa, noticed Cassia lanceolata, Torenia the common Leucas, Bheir, Solanum quercifolia, Banyan, Alstonia, Styrax, Caryota, Elephantopus Osbeckia linearis Herminioides, Wedelia scandens.

At 1,500 feet, Celastrus guttiferoid, Malvacea digyna, of which I found flowers on the path, Kœmpfera terminal, Antidesma, Anthericum, Echites arborea, Careya, Mimosa scandens, Pavetta, Rubiacea alia, Lepidostachys, Lagerstrœmia grandiflora, Leea crispa, Costus, Thunbergia grandiflora, Gordonia, Commelina, Phyllanthus, Briedlia, Dioscorea, Cassia fistula.

As we approached a lower level, the same plants continued : a Dillenia very common, Urena lobata, Hedera terebenthacea : the root is in some cases like figs, Spathodea, Nauclea, Sterculia carnosa, foliis palmatis, Dalbergia, Panax, Semicarpus, Rhaphis trivialis, Cymbid. alvifolium, Sarcanthus guttatus common, Apocynea fauce, 10-glandulata, Ixora, etc.

Saul was not common, nor did I see one tree of any size ; it commenced about the margin of the Toorai.

Among the grasses forming the underwood of the Toorai and the grassy masses clothing the plains, Sacchara were the most common and the most conspicuous : next to these a species of Rottboellia. Sciurus Bengmoria occurred, Hemarthria, Greweia edulis, Leea crispa, Crinum in the Toorai, Viburnum of Sudya, Millingtonia pinnata, Volkameria serrata, Labiata Sudyensis, Mussænda erecta, humilis, Cinchona, Premna herbacea, Phœnix pumila.

Arrived at Chichacootta, a small village, situated in an open grassy plain, miserably stockaded ; and lodged in a good well elevated house.

The following day started and reached Cooch Behar territory, after crossing a considerable but fordable stream. The contrast between the desolate territories of Bootan, and the sheet of cultivation presented by Cooch Behar was striking.

The same contrast continued until we reached the Company's territories, and its less cultivated portions along the bed of the Brahmapootra. The only plant worth notice on the route, was a species of Swertia ; the vegetation being almost precisely the same as in Upper Assam.

Rangamutty, Bhooruwa.

Date.	Station.	Temperature of the air.	Water Boils.					Elevation.		Remarks.
			Large thermometer.	Small metal ditto.	Wooden ditto.	Centigrade ditto.	Woollaston's Ther. Bar.	Determined by the temperature of boiling point.	By Barometer.	
Jan. 27th,	Sassee, ...	62	204½	198	205½	96	6.22.4	4,225	4,325	
,,	Giri Nuddee, lower station, ...	64	206⅕	..	..	..	6.4.3	3,184		
,,	Ditto, upper station,	70	205¾	..	..	..	..	3,450		
29th,	Bailfa, ...	45	200^3	..	201	94	5.9.2			Value of each degree of Centigrade, deduced from difference between this and Sasee, ... 810 ft. Ditto ditto between this and Bailfa, 1,060 ,, Ditto ditto between Sasee and Bailfa, 1,247 ,, 3)3,111 ft. Mean, ... 1,037 ft. But as Sasee and this are correct or nearly so, 810 to be assumed as the right value.

Date.	Station.	Temperature of the air.	Temp. of Boiling point Fahr.	Altitude.		Remarks.
				Det. by Boiling point.	By Bar.	
Jan. 30th,	Bailfa, ...	53	194	....	6804	Each degree is according to this equal to 358 feet 4 inches.
,,	....	45	195	6,764	..	Equivalent each degree to 377 feet 9 inches.
31st,	....	36	195			
,,	Roongdong, ...	..	199	5,175	..	True value of a degree of large Thermometer 398.6 = 398.6.
Feb. 1st,	....	46	199		..	
,,	Benka, ...	64	204	....	..	Assuming 204 as the mean.
2nd,	....	..	204	....	..	
						Value of each degree, deduced from differences in the Barometrical height— Bulfai and Roongdong, .. 408 feet 3 inches. Bulfai and Benka, ... 402 ,, 9 ,, Roongdong and Benka, .. 398 ,, 7 ,, Mean of the three,.. .. 403 feet 2 inches. Value of each degree, deduced from differences in the Thermometer height— Bulfai and Roongdong, .. 387 feet 6 inches. Bulfai and Benka, ... 398 ,, 0 ,, Roongdong and Benka, .. 406 ,, 5 ,, 3)1191 feet 11 inches. Mean, ... 397 feet 3 inches. Mean of both series, .. 403 ,, 2 ,, 2)800 feet 5 inches. True value, ... 400 ,, 2 ,, According to this, this Thermometer will boil at the level of the sea at $211\frac{8}{10}$.

Date.	Station.	Temperature of the air.	Temperature of Boiling point.			Altitude.		Barometer.
			Cent.	Fah.	Wooll.	By Ther.	By Bar.	
2nd,	.. ..	8 P. M. 50	97½	..	627	3,182		
,,	.. ..	4 P. M. 66	..	..	627	....		
,,	.. ..	8½ P. M. 58	..	..	629	....		The cause of the variation in Woollaston's instrument is, I find, the presence of air within the instrument, occupying when the tube is inverted about 2 lines of the tube itself, otherwise it is visible in the bulb. I have therefore taken out the tube and put in a tube from a Centigrade thermometer.
,,	.. ..	8 A. M. 52	..	..	630	....		
3rd,	.. ..	9 P. M. 60	..	..	630	....		
4th,	.. ..	8 A. M. 55	..	..	631	....		
,,	.. ..	12 P. M.	..	..	629	....	.. ..	

Date.	Station.	Temp.	Boiling point Wooll.	Alt. by Boiling point.	Bar. Alt.	Difference.	Remarks.
Feb. 4th,	Benka, 9 P. M. ..	60	755	.. .. ..	3,182		
5th,	,, 7 A. M. ..	..	755				
,,	Monass R., N. Bridge, ..	62	768	1,988 6	1,960	28 6	1,222 feet below Tassgong.
,,	Nulka, ...	68					
,,	Nulka, ...	66	759	2,814 8	2,776	38 8	8 P. M., 8,262 feet above Monass bridge.
6tb,	,, 7 A. M. ..	62	759				
,,	Ghoomkuna, ..	..	760				
,,	Bridge over Koollong, ..	..	757	.. .. ..	2,430		
,,	Khumna, ..	..	742				
,,	.. .. ..	..	$742\frac{5}{10}$	4,360 1	4,292	68 1	1,557-6, above Nulka; 2,386-8, above Monass bridge.
7th,	Phoollong, ..	..	$736\frac{5}{10}$	5,830	5,929	99 0	4 P. M. The scale is now fastened so that the Vernier corresponds to the lower mark and to the first division above Zero, hence to equalize them, it must be subtracted from all, after to-day.
8th,	,, in doors 47,	47	$736\frac{5}{10}$	Mean, 737			
	,, out 39,	39					
,,	,, ...	..	738				

Date.	Station.	Temp.	Ther.	Altitude.	Bar. Alt.	Difference.	Remarks.
Feb. 9th,	Phoollong, ..	35	736 $\frac{5}{10}$				
,,	,, 9 P. M. ..	46	741				
10th,	Tassyassa, 4½ P. M.	60	742	.. ..	.. ..	.. ..	Mean deduced from 4 series 91 $\frac{5}{10}$ (P.)
,,	,, 9 P. M. ..	52	743 5	Mean from comparisons with all,			
11th,	,, 9 A. M. ..	42	744				
,,	,, 12 P. M. ..	56	743 5	5,206	5,272	.. ..	91 $\frac{3}{10}$
,,	,, 4 P. M. ..	60	743				
,,	,, 9 P. M. ..	50	745	....	.. ..	.. ..	
12th,	,, 10 A. M. ..	48	745	....	.. ..	.. ..	
,,	,, 12 P. M. ..	54	743	....	.. ..	.. ..	743-8 is the mean.
,,	,, 4 P. M. ..	51	744 5	....	.. ..	.. ..	
,,	,, 9 P. M. ..	49	745	....	.. ..	.. ..	
13th,	,, 10¾ A. M. ..	48	744 5	....	.. ..	.. ..	
,,	,, 12½ P. M. ..	57	742 5	....	.. ..	.. ..	
14th,	,, 7 A. M. ..	43					
,,	Sanah, 4 P. M ..	51	716 5				
,,	,, 9 P. M. ..	50	719	7,845	7,983	138	Storm threatening.
15th,	,, 6 A. M. ..	46	717 5				
,,	1st Hill, ...	..	705	9,078			
,,	2nd Ditto, ...	39	681	11,269			
,,	Summit, ...	..	667 5	12,477			
16th,	Halt, ...	..	699	....	9,602		
,,	Linjai, ...	51	734				
17th,	,, 10 A. M. ..	54	735	6,385	6,335	50	
,,	,, 12 P. M. ..	55	734 5				
,,	,, 4½ P. M. ..	54	734				
18th,	Kooree, ...	1¼	760 5				
,,	,, Bridge, ..	1¼	761	3,878 5			
19th,	Ling-ling, 11½ A.M.	52	752 5				
,,	,, 1 P. M. ..	53 5	752 5	4,601	4,522	79	
,,	,, 4 P. M. ..	53 5	752 5				Cloudy, threatening day.
20th,	,, 10 A. M. ..	54	755	....	....	....	Fine.
,,	,, ,, ..	55	753 5				

,,	,, 4 P. M. ..	57	753 5					
21st,	,, 11 A. M.	56	754 5	....	.. ....	....	....	Cloudy, raw day, especially towards evening.
,,	,, 4 P. M. ..	55	753	....	.. ....	....	....	
22nd,	,, 10½ A. M.	54	754 5	....	.. ....	....	....	Cloudy, and apparently snowing all around; same raw weather.
,,	,, 4 P. M. ..	55	754	....	.. ..	....	....	
23rd,	Greatest height, ..	..	734		6,211			
,,	Tumashoo, 4 P. M.	55	747	....	.. ..	....	....	Cloudy, raw, threatening day.
,,	,, 8⅓ A. M.	56	749		5,022	5,012		
24th,	,, 7 A. M.	54	749	....	..			
,,	1st Ravine, ...	65	749 5		4,886	4,807	....	Fine day, thunder at 3 P. M., Rain in evening; snow falling on heights around.
,,	Gratst. ht. 2¼ P.M.	58	724 5		7,169	7,272	....	
,,	Oongar, 5 P. M...	58	734		6,256	6,371	....	Rainy and threatening, ditto ditto.
25th,	,, 9 P. M...	54	735					
,,	Oongar Brg. 12½ P. M.	..	744		5,366	5,381	....	Rainy, cloudy weather.
,,	Ascent 1st Stat. ..	..	717		7,853	... .	....	Cloudy with showers.
,,	Pémee, 8 P. M...	..	702 5					
26th,	,, 8 A. M. ..	..	702		9,197	9,692	....	Cloudy and misty.
,,	Rodoola Peak, ..	..	672		1,200 3	12,335	....	Ditto ditto.
,,	Bhoomlung-tung, 8 P. M.	..	713					
27th,	,, 11 A. M. ..	46	713		8,570 3	8,668	8,668	Sunny. Cloudy occasionally. Sunny.
,,	,, 4 P. M. ..	..	709					
28th,	,, 11 A. M. ..	51	711 5					
,,	,, 4 P. M. ..	53	711					
,,	Ridge above Byagur,	..	....	....	.. ....	9,947	....	Broken.
March 2nd,	Byagur, 4 P. M...	50	569 5		569 2 5	8,149	8,149	New tube, 54 5 8=558
3rd,	,, 9 A. M. ..	45	569			.. ....	....	Tassgong, ... 658=3,182
,,	,, 10 A. M...	60	569			.. ....	....	Byagur, ... 569=8,149
								89=4,967= 55 8
,,	,, 9 P. M. ..	45	569 5					Tassangsee, 623, ... 59 7
4th,	Summit, ...	48	539		1,114 9	11,035	11,099	
,,	Nullah, ...	49	552		987	9,642	9,810	Mean, ... 57 7
,,	Jaisa, ...	..	556					
,,	,, ...	..	555 5		555 8 1	9,410	9,444	Byagur and Tongsa.
5th,	,, 7 A. M. ..	..	556					

Date.	Station.	Temp.	Ther.	Altitude.	Bar. Alt.	Difference.	Remarks.
March 5th,	Summit, 12½ P.M.	..	538	....	10,931	11,204	Byagur, Jaisa, and Tongsa.
,,	Ravine, 3 P.M. ..	..	562 5	....	8,473	8,737	Ditto ditto ditto.
6th	Tongsa, 10 A. M.	53	585 5	....			
,,	,, 4 P. M. ..	58 5	585	....			Sunny day with passing clouds.
7th,	,, 11 A. M. ..	53	585	....	6,527	6,588	Sunny day, deduced from Jaisa and Byagur.
,,	,, 4 P. M. ..	..	585	....			Cloudy.
8th,	,, 10 A. M. ..	53	586	....			
9th,	,, 11 A. M. ..	55	585				
,,	,, 4½ P.M. ..	60	585 5				
10th,	,, 10½ A. M.	53	585 5				
,,	,, 4 P. M. ..	53	583	....	....	... ...	Raw, cloudy day.
11th,	,, 11 A. M. ..	51 5	584 5	....	....	... ...	Fine weather, snow around at night.
,,	,, 4 P. M. ..	59	583 5				
12th,	,, 11 A. M ..	52	584				
13th,	,, 10½ A. M.	53	584 5				
,,	,, 4 P. M. ..	58	584				
14th,	,, 10½ A. M.	52	585	....	....	....	Fine.
,,	,, 4 P. M. ..	62	583 5				
15th,	,, 10½ A. M.	55	585	....	....	....	Fine.
,,	,, 4 P. M. ..	60	584 5	....	....	....	Cloudy.
16th,	,, ...	56	585				
17th,	,, 10 A. M. ..	55 5	585				Fine.
,,	,, 4 P. M ..	59	583 5				Cloudy, rain throughout night.
18th,	,, 10½ A.M. ..	55	586				Cloudy.
,,	,, 11 A.M. ..	58	586				Fine.
19th,	,, 10 A. M. ..	54	587	584 9	6,588	6,527	Cloudy, threatening.
,,	,, 4 P. M. .	58	585				Cloudy, slight rain.
20th,	,, 10 A. M. ..	54	587				Ditto.
,,	,, 4 P. M. ..	62	584 5				Fine.
21st,	,, 10 A. M. ..	55	586				Cloudy, rain in the morning.
,,	,, 4 P. M. ..	57	585				
23rd,	,, Bridge, ..	63	599	5	5,154	5,417	— 263. Rain.
,,	Taseeling, 4 P.M.	..	576	576 7 5	7,358	7,233	+ 125.
24th,	,, 7½ P.M. ..	..	577				

,,	Pagoda, 2⅓ P. M.	..	572	....	..	....	7,829	7,602	+ 227.
25th,	Chinduj. 10 A. M.	51	571		571 5		7,875	7,863	+ 122.
,,	,, 4 P. M. ..	59	572	....	..	....	....	....	Confluence of Gnee and Roogoon, 8,213.
26th,	Summit, ...	48	540 5	....	..	....	10,955	10,873	+ 82.
,,	Rydang, 4½ P. M.	58	579	{ ..	579 2 5		7,110	6,965	+ 145.
27th,	,, 8 A. M. ..	59	579 5						
,,	Ridge, 12½ P. M.	..	566 5	....	..	....	8,374	8,308	— 66.
,,	Santagong, 9 P. M.	..	587	....	..	....	6,276	6,325	— 49.
28th,	Thain, 4 P. M. ..	..	599						
30th,	,, 10 A. M. ..	62	599 5		598 4		5,213	5,279	Cloudy, — 66.
,,	,, 4 P. M. ..	61	598	....	..	....	....	....	Cloudy, windy.
31st,	,, 10 A. M. ..	60 5	597	....	..	....	....	....	Fine.
April 2nd,	Punukha, 10 A. M.	68	617 5						
,,	,, 4 P. M. ..	73	614 5	....	..	....	....	3,640	— 617·5, windy.
,,	,, 12 P. M. ..	..	615		3,654				
3rd,	,, 10 A. M. ..	69	617	....	..	....	....	....	Fine.
,,	,, 12 P. M. ..	75	615 5						
,,	,, 4 P. M. ..	78	613	....	..	....	....	....	Cloudy, windy. Thermometer at 2½ P. M. 82°.
4th,	,, 10½ A. M.	72	614 5	....	..	....	....	....	Fine.
,,	,, 4 P. M. ..	77	612	....	..	....	3,789	....	Cloudy, windy.
5th,	,, 10½ A. M.	71	615	....	..	....	....	....	Cloudy, calm.
,,	,, 4 P. M. ..	72	611 5	....	..	....	....	....	Stormy, slight rain, violent wind SW., 9 P. M. 68° 5′.
6th,	,, 10½ A. M. ..	66 5	614 5	....	..	....	....	....	Calm, fine, 8 A. M. 63°.
,,	,, 12 P. M. ..	68	614	....	..	....	....	....	Ditto ditto.
,,	,, 4 P. M. .	70	614	....	..	....	....	....	Cloudy, rain at 2½ P. M., 9 P. M. 65°
7th,	,, 10 A. M.	65	615	....	..	....	....	....	Calm and fine, 8 A. M. 63° 5′.
,,	,, 12 P. M. ..	73	613	....	..	....	....	....	Windy.
,,	,, 4 P. M. ..	70 5	613	....	..	....	....	....	Windy and cloudy, 9½ P. M. 68°.
8th,	,, 11 A. M. ..	66	614	....	..	....	....	....	8 A. M. 64°, hazy, calm.
,,	,, 4 P. M. ..	68 5	612	....	..	....	....	....	Windy, rain—rain at night.
9th,	,, 10 A. M. ..	64	615	....	..	....	....	....	8 A. M. 61° 5′, fine, very clear
,,	,, 12¼ P. M.	70	614	....	..	....	....	....	Fine and calm.
,,	,, 4 P. M. ..	71	613 5	....	..	....	....	....	Rain, windy, 9 P. M. 68°, cloudy.
10th,	,, 4 P. M. ..	66	....	....	..	....	....	....	Overcast, rain during night, 8 A. M. 63°, 9 P. M. 43° 5.
11th,	,, 10½ A. M.	65	614 5	....	..	....	....	....	Cloudy, calm, showers, drizzling yesterday.
,,	,, 12 P. M. ..	66	614	....	..	....	....	....	Ditto ditto.
,,	,, 4 P. M. ..	67	612	....	..	....	....	....	Ditto ditto, 9 P. M. 66°, very cloudy.

Date.	Station	Temp.	Ther.	Altitude.	Bar. Alt.	Difference.	Remarks.
April 12th,	Punukha, 10 A. M.	66	613	....	....	....	8 A. M. 62°, calm and fine, very cloudy.
,,	,, 4 P. M. ..	72 5	611 5	....	....	....	Cloudy, windy, 9½ P. M. 68° 5', cloudy.
13th,	,, 10½ A. M.	70	614	....	....	....	8 A. M. 68°, fine ditto ditto.
,,	,, 12 P. M. ..	76	611	....	....	....	Wind getting up.
,,	,, 4 P. M. ..	79 8	612	....	....	....	Cloudy, windy, violent wind from NW. at 5 P. M.
14th,	,, 10 A. M. ..	67 5	615	....	....	....	8 A. M. 65°, rather cloudy, ditto ditto.
,,	,, 12 P. M. ..	69 8	612	....	....	....	Cloudy, close.
,,	,, 4 P. M. ..	74	611	....	....	....	Violent wind, thermometer 3½ P. M. 67° 8'.
15th,	,, 10½ A. M.	66	614 5	....	....	....	8 A. M. 62°, fine and calm, ditto.
,,	,, 12 P. M. ..	76	612 5	....	....	....	Cloudy, but calm, strong wind from usual direction
,,	,, 4 P. M. ..	71 5	613 5				[at 1.
16th,	,, 10 A. M. ..	-66	614	....	....	....	Fine.
,,	,, 4 P. M. ..	72	612	....	....	....	Cloudy, calm, strong W. wind at 1-3.
17th,	,, 10 A. M. ..	65	....	....	....	....	Broken.
,,	,, 12 P. M. ..	71 5	....	....	....	....	Cloudy, calm, slight shower at 6 A. M.
,,	,, 8 P. M. ..	66					
18th,	,, 8 A. M. ..	64	....	3,739			
,,	,, 10 A. M. ..	67	....				
,,	,, 12 P. M. ..	74	....	....	....	....	Windy, rather cloudy.
,,	,, 4 P. M. ..	75	....	....	....	....	Ditto ditto ditto.
19th,	,, 8 A. M. ..	67	....	....	....	....	Cloudy.
,,	,, 10 A. M. ..	69	....	....	....	....	Ditto
,,	,, 12 P. M. ..	73	....	....	....	....	Clouds and sun, wind rising.
,,	,, 4 P. M. ..	74	....	....	....	....	Cloudy, very windy.
,,	,, 9½ P. M.	70	....	....	....	....	Very bright, clouds as usual from N.
20th,	,, 8 A. M. ..	69	....	....	....	....	Fine.
,,	,, 10 A. M. ..	72	....	....	....	....	Passing clouds.
,,	,, 12 P. M. ..	74	....	....	....	....	Cloudy and windy.
,,	,, 4 P. M. ..	78	....	....	....	....	Ditto.
,,	,, 9½ P. M. ..	70	....	....	....	....	Cloudy.
21st,	,, 8 A. M. ..	69	....	....	....	....	Fine and cloudy.

Date.	Time.	Temp.	Remarks.
April 21st,	10 A. M. ..	72	Fine, some clouds.
,,	12 P. M. ..	78	Fine, windy.
,,	4 P. M. ..	80	Cloudy, very windy.
,,	10 P. M. ..	73	Rather cloudy.
22nd,	8 A. M. ..	71	Fine, sultry.
,,	12 P. M. ..	80	Rather cloudy, gusts of wind.
,,	4 P. M. ..	78	Slight rain, windy, at 7½ P. M.
23rd,	8 A. M. ..	72	Fine.
,,	10 A. M. ..	73	
,,	4 P. M. ..	81	Windy and cloudy.
,,	11 P. M. ..	71	Rain at 9 P. M
24th,	8 A. M. ..	68	
,,	10 A. M. ..	70	Fine and calm.
,,	4 P. M. ..	82	Fine, windy.
,,	11 P. M. ..	73	
25th,	8 A. M. ..	70	
,,	10 A. M. ..	72	Calm.
,,	12 P. M. ..	79	Wind getting up.
,,	4 P. M. ..	82	Windy.
,,	8 P. M. ..	75	Windy, hazy.
26th,	8 A. M. ..	70	Hazy.
,,	10 A M. ..	72	Calm, sultry.
,,	4 P. M. ..	81	Windy.
,,	8 P. M. ..	78	Windy, till 9 or 9½ P. M.
27th,	8 A. M. ..	73	Sultry, hazy.
,,	10 A. M. ..	74	Ditto ditto.
,,	12½ P. M. ..	82	Ditto ditto.
,,	4 P. M. ..	83	Ditto ditto, windy.
,,	11 P. M. ..	76	Ditto ditto, fine.
28th,	8 A. M. ..	72	Sultry.
,,	10½ A. M.	75	Ditto.
,,	4 P. M. ..	83	Wind violent.
,,	10 P. M. ..	75	Cloudy.
29th,	8 A. M. ..	70	Cloudy, hazy, sultry.
,,	10 A. M. ..	75	
,,	12 P. M. ..	79	
,,	4 P. M. ..	78	Hazy, less windy.
,,	10 P. M. ..	73	Cloudy, rain at 8 P. M.
30th,	8 A. M. ..	70	Cloudy.
,,	10 A. M. ..	71	Cloudy and hazy.
,,	12 P. M. ..	74	Close.
,,	4 P. M. ..	76	Windy, very hazy.
,,	9 P. M. ..	73	
,,	10 P. M. ..	73	Cloudy.
May 1st,	8 A. M. ..	71	Hazy, sultry.
,,	10 A. M. ..	71	Cool, cloudy.
,,	12 P. M. ..	72	Ditto ditto.
,,	4 P. M. ..	75	No wind to 6½ P. M.
,,	8 P. M. ..	73	Cloudy.
,,	10½ P. M.	73	Ditto.
2nd,	8 A. M. ..	70	Cloudy and hazy.
,,	10 A. M. ..	73	
,,	12 P. M. ..	75	
,,	4 P. M. ..	75	Usual wind about 5 P. M.
,,	10 P. M. ..	73	Much less violent.
3rd,	8 A. M. ..	71	Cloudy.
,,	10 A. M. ..	73	Fine, cloudy and windy since 12 P. M.
,,	12 P. M. ..	75,5	
,,	4 P M. ..	79	

Date.	Time.	Temp.	Remarks.
May 3rd,	10 P. M. ..	73	Cloudy.
4th,	8 A. M. ..	71	Cloudy, rain at night.
,,	10 A. M. ..	73	Cloudy, wind getting up.
,,	4 P. M. ..	75	Cloudy, rather windy.
5th,	8 A. M. ..	71	Cloudy, rain.
,,	10 A. M. ..	72	Ditto ditto.
,,	12 P. M. ..	72	Cloudy, close.
,,	4 P. M. ..	76	Fine, rather windy.
,,	8½ P. M.	71	Cloudy.
6th,	8 A. M. ..	72	Fine, sultry.
,,	10 A. M. ..	73	Ditto ditto.
,,	12½ P. M.	80	Windy, fine.
,,	4 P. M. ..	76	Windy, clouds flying.
,,	.. ..	..	Clouds.
7th,	8 A. M. ..	72	Fine.
,,	10 A. M. ..	74	Ditto.
,,	,, ...	79	Violent gusts from west with dust.
11th,	7 A. M. ..	51	